Khosrow and Shirin

by Hatifi (Author) and Suzi (Illustrator)

Annotated 2026 edition with reformatted artwork and print of the original manuscript and English translation

For information contact: www.perennifolio.com
Instagram: @perennifoliopress
Facebook: @perennifolio
Linkedin: www.linkedin.com/perennifolio

ISBN: 979-8-90290-004-7

Credits:
Cover Design: Perennifolio Press
Front Cover Art: Inside illustration from Khosrow and Shirin, the copy exhibited at Metropolitan Museum of Art and digitized in Public Domain.
Back Cover Art: Portrait of Hatifi by Kamāl ud-Dīn Behzād, Public Domain.
Editorial Revisions and Additions: Perennifolio Press
Interior Art and Manuscript Editions: Perennifolio Press
Translation: Perennifolio Press and Chat GPT Collaboration

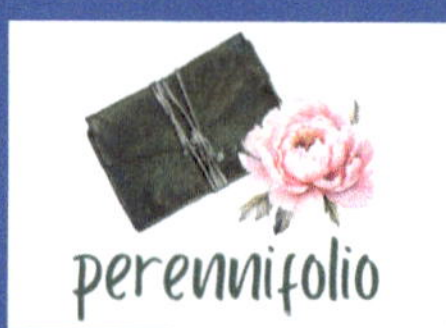

Khosrow and Shirin

by Hatifi (Author) and Suzi (Illustrator)

Annotated 2026 edition with reformatted artwork and print of the original manuscript and English translation

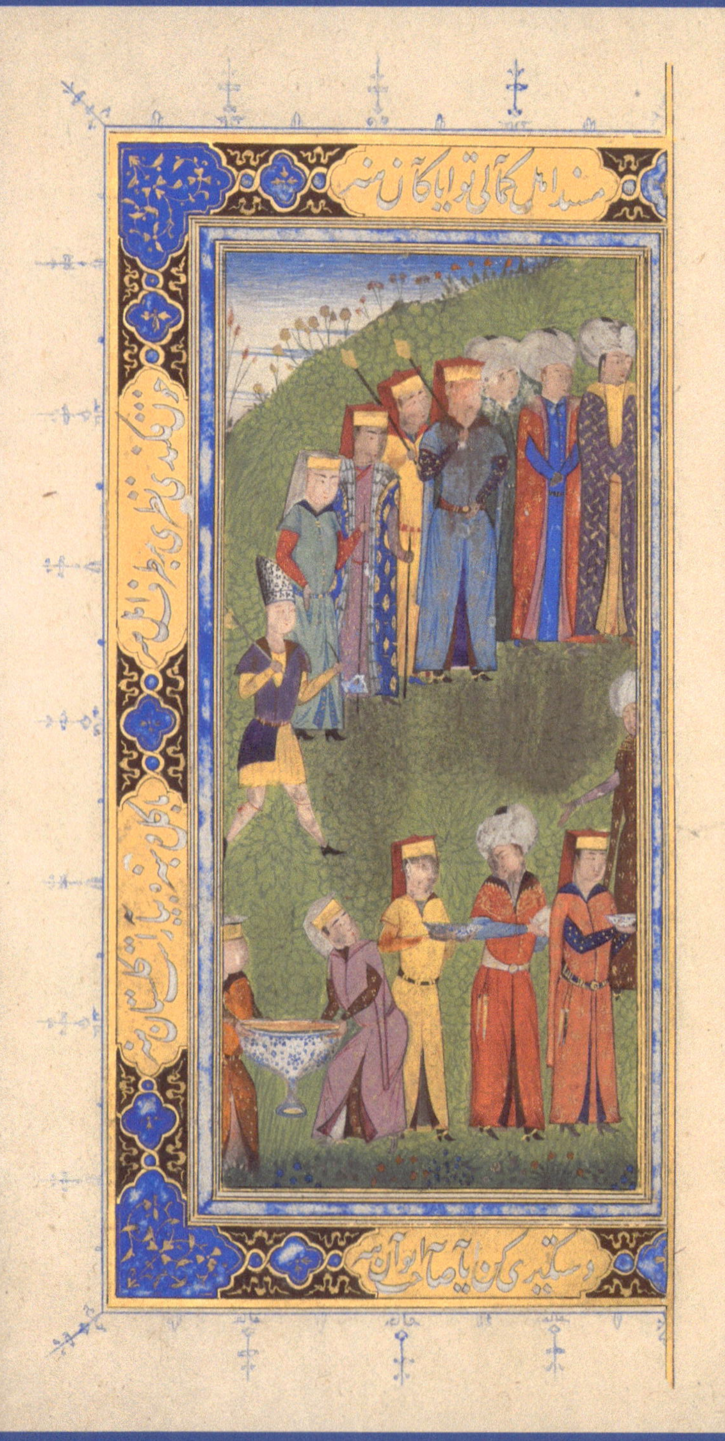

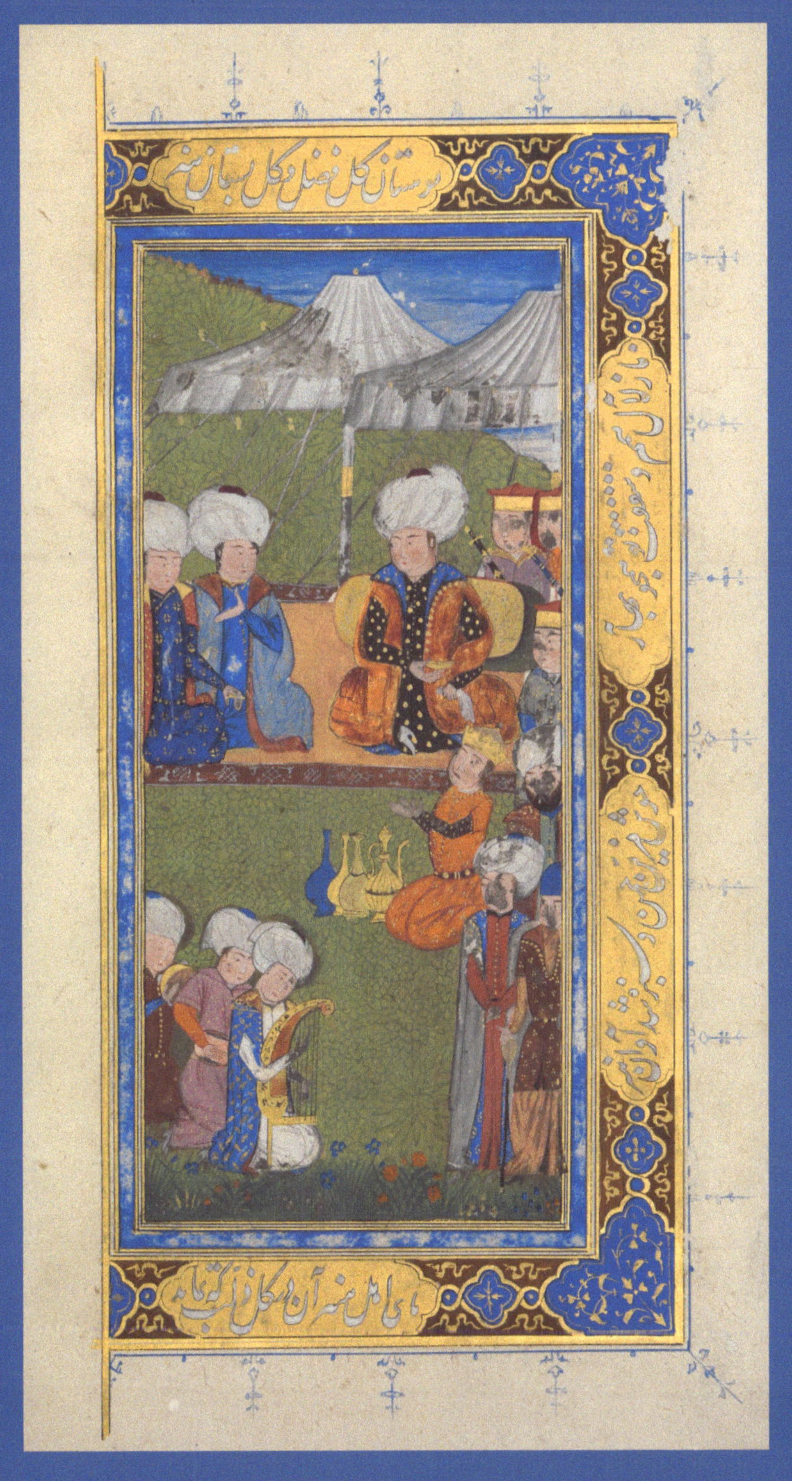

Inscriptions on Page 1 includes the following translation:

Top Caption (Scene Title): Arrival of Khosrow
at the royal hunting ground.

Right Vertical Caption: Khosrow arrives with his companions
at the hunting fields.

Bottom Caption: Servants bring wine and food,
preparing the royal gathering in the field.

Miniature content includes a scene with royal pavilion, Khosrow as King, hosting a hunting event followed with a food banquet.

Page 2 inscriptions includes the following translation:

Top Caption: When Khosrow sent him into that pavilion,
he seated him before him in his royal gathering.

Right Vertical Caption: Khosrow seated in the banquet
with musicians and performers.

Bottom Caption: The king's banquet with musicians and entertainers.

Miniature content includes a scene with royal pavilion, Khosrow as King, hosting a musical banquet following the hunting event.

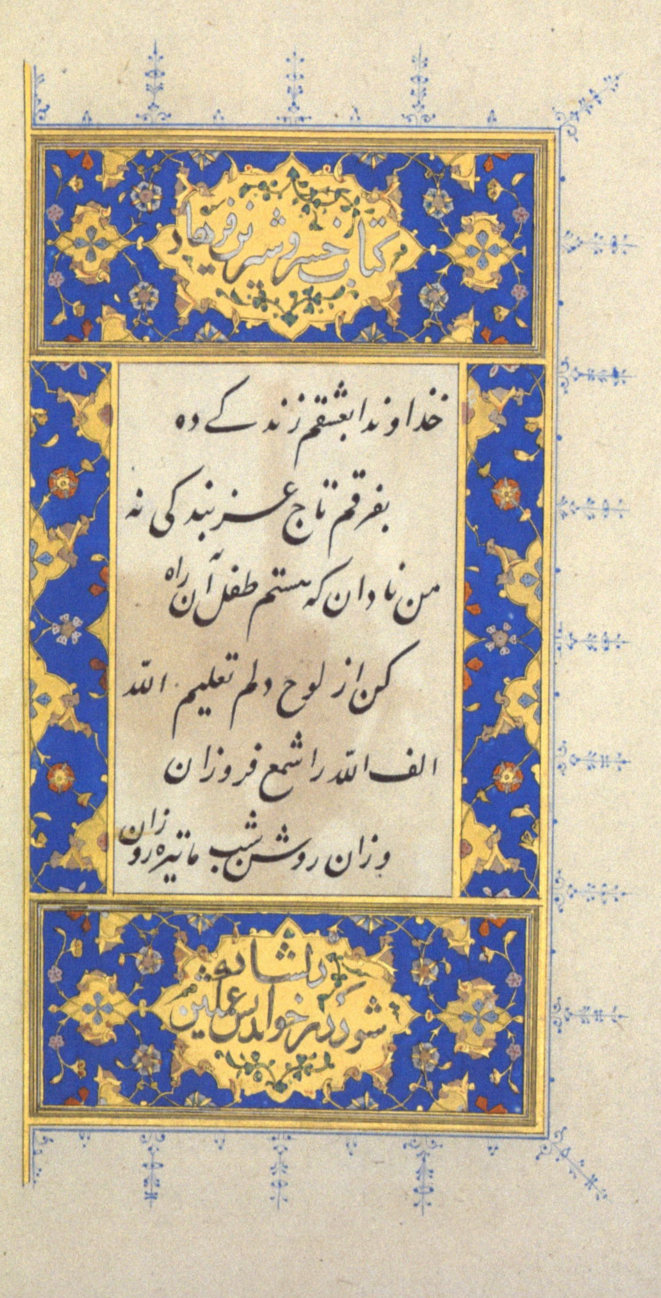

کتاب خسرو شیرین فرهاد

خداوندا بعشقم زندگی ده
بفرقم تاج عز بندگی نه
من نادان که هستم طفل آن راه
کن از لوح دلم تعلیم الله
الف الله را شمع فروزان
وزان روشن شب ماتیره روزان

Page 5 includes three textual layers:

1. Top illuminated title cartouche (rubric)
2. Central poem panel (main narrative verses)
3. Bottom illuminated title cartouche (next section heading)

Translation of these pieces is as follows:

Top Rubric:
The Tale of Khosrow and Farhad.

Central Poem Panel:
The Lord who gives and who creates,
To every people He grants the crown of honor,
I and all part of my being exist by the decree of His royal seal,
I inscribe the tablet of my heart with the name of the All-Knowing,
For the wise read in that sacred alphabet,
The hidden knowledge of the world.

Bottom Rubric:
Concerning Farhad's love and his seeing of Shirin

بیا ای طوطی فکرت سخن گوی
که میگردد بکامت این کهن گوی

برای خامهٔ این ره را بتارک
که آمد این سفر بر ما مبارک

ز هر حرفی که گردی نکته پرداز
بنام ایزد بیچون کن آغاز

افتتاح نامه بنام پادشاهی که اورنگ نشینان تاج بخش
محتاج وار بر خاک احتیاج نشسته راه او دیده مستغنیان بارگاه
استغنا کمر بندگی بر میان ادب بسته جویان ظل سا و دولت او

بنام آنکه جان را زندگی داد
وزان پس مژدهٔ پایندگی داد

نفس را قوتش از حرف جانبخش
زبان را از نفس حکمت روان بخش

خرد بخشید تا او را بدانیم
ز گرد غیر او دامن فشانیم

ز قرآن داد ما را پیشگاهی
که هر سطرش بمقصود است راهی

ز باغ صنع او طوبی نهالی
ز کلک او سواد دهر خالی

بر آب از آدمی زد نقش زیبا
که باقی ماند همچون نقش دیبا

گرفت از پنجهٔ خورشید ناخن
که پستان ماه نو ابروی خود کن

Page 7 includes a Rubric Heading in gold ink that reads: The story of Farhad and Shirin and the expression of their love.

Translation of the top and bottom part of the poetic narrative is as follows:

By the blessing of a noble spirit,
His soul was shaped in purity and light.
The gates of both worlds opened before him,
And destiny lifted its pen to begin his tale.
Wisdom kept him company,
And knowledge brightened every word he spoke.
His speech carried elegance and warmth,
His thoughts moved with quiet understanding.
From his tongue flowed living fountains of speech,
And in his mind the gardens of insight bloomed.

These verses appear to introduce the character of Farhad.

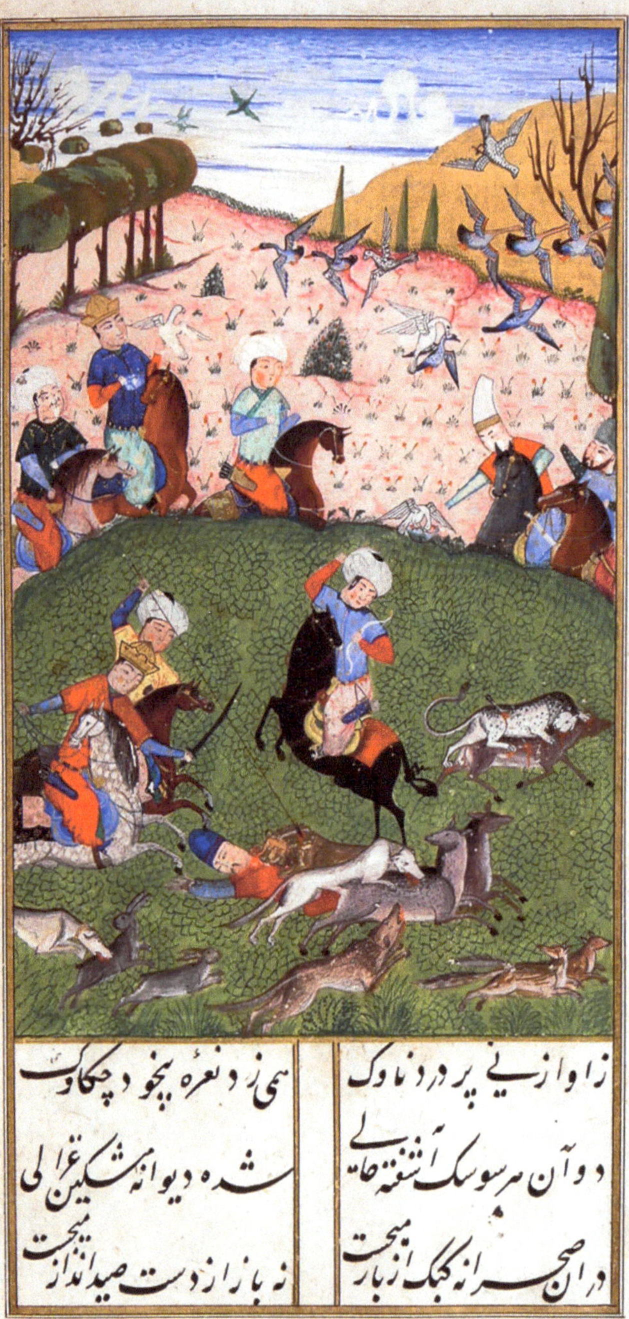
ز آواز نی پر درد ناوک
همی زد نعره پنجود چکاوک
دو آن هر سو سگ آشفته حالی
شده دیوانه مشکین غزالی
در آن صحرا نه کبک از بار محنت
نه باز از دست صیدانداز محنت

Page 9 includes a hunting scenery with Khosrow which includes a poem panel with the following literary translation in a longer 16-line iteration:

The air rang with the clamor of armor and arrows,
And riders spurred their horses in restless motion.
Each lord pressed forward from his station,
Eager for the moment of the strike.

Like larks startled into flight,
The nobles gathered before the field of sport.
From the yellow-clawed falcons the prey was driven out,
And one by one the hunters cast their birds to the wind.

The king rode at the center of the chase—
His horse rearing above the fleeing herd.
Deer scattered across the green hillside
While arrows and talons fell among them.

Around him the hunt unfolded in widening circles:
Falcons stooping from the sky,
Riders leaning from their saddles,
And the plain alive with the thunder of pursuit.

جادو خرام را بجولان دادن شبدیز زیبا رفتار قید کردن

کمند انداز این صید کهن دشت / درین وادی کمند زین گونه گلگشت

که خسرو با پری رویان نیمراد / زعیش و شادمانی خرم و شاد

شدش روزی هوای صید نخجیر / که بامشکین غزالان افکند تیر

هوای خرم و فصل بهاران / نشانده ابر گرد ره زباران

نشسته آفتاب دی بزردی / شده باغ از بنفشه لاجوردی

ززیر ژاله رسته سبزه تر / چنان کز بیضه طوطی برزند سر

میان لاله ع ع جا گرفته / چو خوبان پای در حنا گرفته

شده از اعتدال باد نوروز / در و دیوار گیتی خاطر افروز

چو زیر آب گشته عسه برف / شده عکس گلش لمعای شنگرف

گل کاهی زکوی غنچهٔ تر / نشانده بر گریبان تکمه زر

ز بهر عشرت گلهای خود فام / چمن را خانه بلبل شده جام

شده زیر شگوفه نخل تر گم / زگرمان بارگون پوشیده قاقم

Page 11 includes two panels of the storyline from the manuscript. This is the first next available page from the public domain pages digitized. The storyline here seems to have progressed into the description of the beauty of the Shirin. The expanded literary translation is as follows:

Opening Header:
When Zuhra gladdened me with words she spoke,
The king's own heart with that same joy awoke.

Right Column:
He said to me: "Approve not such a nature,
For men are placed beside the poor as partners".
The brightness of his white hair then appeared;
Toward friend and foe alike his course he steered.
A somber robe upon his shoulders lay,
And darker still it seemed beneath the gaze.
Among the tulip-cheeked he took his place;
His balanced grace lit every heart with light.
Seated upon the pulpit he remained,
Like sorrow's garden folded in a bud.
Above the bud the famed and fragrant flowers
Yet from the eye their brightness slowly dimmed.

Left Column:

Within these two tales mark what he has said
Of love and passion, grace and open hand.
Though all this speech he did not wholly give,
He set its language deep within the heart.
The garden freshened, radiant and new;
Through love it filled with fragrance and with bloom.
As though a parrot suddenly had flown,
Like a nightingale bereft of its tree.
The doors and walls rose upward all around;
No image of those wondrous flowers remained.
Seated upon a throne where tears might fall,
The turning sky would never serve as cup.
Now look—at last the destined rank is reached.

نشان خیمهٔ عشرت شده گل
مقرر گشته عشرتگاه بلبل

شده قمری برافغان گرم از شوق
بدیده آورده از قوس قزح طوق

شراب ارغوانی لاله در سر
لباس شادمانی غنچه در بر

ز هر سو غنچهٔ رعنای لاله
شده کام غزالان را نواله

هوای معتدل نی گرم و نی سرد
نه دشواری گل و نه محنت ورد

زمین زان می که خورد از جام گردون
ز سبزه رنگ دل میداد بیرون

ریاحین تا ز روی سبزه نوخیز
سوی صحرا جنیبت راند پرویز

پری رویان نگار و رهای تازی
همی راندند پیشانیش بازی

نگارین لعبتان پرنیان پوش
همه آشوب عقل و آفت هوش

همه در جلوه گرد اگرد خسرو
کواکب وار بر گرد مه نو

کمانها کیانی بر سر دست
از آن صید افکنان صیدی نمیجست

یکی میکرد بال کلنک آماج
یکی میبست بر فتراک دراج

خدنگی هر طرف گردیده سروی
هما کش مانده هر جانب تذروی

Page 14 includes two panels of the storyline from the manuscript. It is the continuation of the previous page.

The literary translation is as follows:

Right Column:

From my lord's favor the servant's heart found honor;
Fortune itself rose high in the heavens of truth.
A draught of spirit-wine for the tulip-faced beloved
Seized the whole kingdom of the heart with love.
The air of the gathering grew warm and sweet;
Time and the earth adorned themselves for joy.
Thus the meadow's face turned bright with green,
And wide the watching eyes were opened.
At moments the nightingales spread their wings there,
While nature girded itself for delight.
As though one asked: where and when shall this appear?
Then suddenly a herald entered the garden,
And a hundred faces turned toward him

Left Column:

Love was proclaimed and changed all things;
The wind of fortune lifted its wings.
Sorrow fled entirely from the scene,
And no moment lingered silent.
Neither the flower's pride nor its delight remained—
All lived united and fortunate.
Speech awakened what had long been sleeping;
Never had one seen such a falcon.
From you as well came wisdom's confession,
While branch and leaf bore fruit together.
From that hunt they fell to rest;
The night grew harder than ivory.
No man could capture its reflection.

ز بهر صید آن شهزاده تا شب — جنیبت راند با خیل شکرلب

شبانگاه کاین گردیده گرداب — چو آب زندگی گردید نایاب

زمانه از سیاهی شب داج — رقم زد بر بیاض تخته عاج

جهان تاریک شد بر چشم مردم — ز تاریکی شب گردید ره گم

قضا را ز آتشی بنمود از دور — شد آتش دیده پرویز را نور

نمود آن قوم را آتش گلستان — سوی آتش شدند آتش پرستان

دهی بود اندران ده جا گرفتند — بعشرت ساغر صهبا گرفتند

ببانگ ارغنون و ناله چنگ — روان گردید جام ارغوان رنگ

چو مطرب زخمه بر عود میزد — صدایش طعنه بر طنبور میزد

نی نایی نکو نیم نیشکر بود — ز نیشکر چو شیرین کاربر بود

دران شب بود نقل باده خوران — همه بادام چشم گلعذاران

گهی سیب ذقن که شکرلب — گزیدی چون گزک مستان دران شب

بعشرت آتشابان بودند تا روز — ز تاب آتش می مجلس افروز

Page 17 includes two panels of the storyline from the manuscript. It is the continuation of the previous page. The literary translation is as follows:

Right Column:

To guard his purpose he hastened on;
The king in haste beheld delight and life.
With the first breath of morning's wind
The whole wide world seemed lifted up anew.
Fate with a finger showed its hidden secret—
The heart itself commanded fire to rise.
Nothing from him was given save the hour:
Desert, assembly, and the tumult joined.
The search for the maiden then appeared,
And judge and witness both declared it so.
That night the message came to him:
"This craft does not tremble or fail."
In honor firm, he bore the insult still.

Left Column:

Your beauty—though the wounded heart endures—
Is like the water of life within the eyes.
His anger mingled strangely into love;
Life's darkened night left sight grown dim.
The fire rose fierce and powerful within;
Toward the flame no outward sign remained.
At dawn the breath of paradise returned,
And tears like flowing streams filled up the eyes.
A hundred thoughts were scattered to the wind,
Yet joy appeared again upon a day.
The heavens turned their circling beads above,
Like the revolving dome that follows the sun.
But still the tongue of slander rose against him.

شوی گرد ره سویش نیابی غباری از سر کویش نیابی

بود قصری که آن مه را مقامست که خشت پخته اش از سیم خامست

منقش پیکری موزون و سنگین وزو هر خانه شش بیت رنگین

سپهر نیلگون نیلین رواقش بود قوس قزح عکسی ز طاقش

زند ایوان و طاق او ره دین چو پیشانی و ابروی بت چین

گچ و خاکش که بنا کرد تخمیر بهم آمیخته چون شکر و شیر

بود از تیشهای تا ندانش دل نازک چو خوبان جهانش

خط القاب کرد هر رواقی چو خط بر گرد روی سیم ساقی

کشاده دیده هر جانب ز روزن شده حیران خود زان چشم روشن

لب هر صفه شیرینیست خندان نموده از صف دندانه دندان

بود هر کنگرش دست دعایی که نبود در وی الا دلربایی

خلد از کنگرش در پهلوی ماه کمند حیله را زان دست کوتاه

بود دیوار آن از سنگ مرمر که می لغزد ز یادش پای صرصر

Page 20 includes two panels of the storyline from the manuscript. The story seems to have progresed from the previous page made available in public domain. The literary translation is as follows:

Right Column:
Become not dust along the ants' low road,
For even palaces may harbor harm.
The pattern of the sky, the weight of heaven,
Holds earth and flame together in its form.
Youth is not born from fire alone—
So guard the covenant of eye and gaze.
The turning of the heart's steep path brought pain;
A message line was sent by one unknown.
He turned and placed that letter in my hand,
And suddenly the page itself seemed bright.
Within love's snare a whispered prayer arose—
His sorrowed face shone pale like moonlight,
And from that moon the fire of love leapt forth.

Left Column:

His dust lay softly in the water of the lane;
His nature finer still than molten silver.
He sat as though beneath the star of Venus,
Content within the circle of his speech.
His silver arms were folded close about him,
As though he drank a burning draught of flame.
Within that street what tale, what flowing water—
A line traced gently round a silver face.
His motion flowed, ensnared within the field;
He tasted praise in sight of the beloved.
Now two bright faces shine like twin suns;
Each secret of the heart is told in whispers.
And words grow sweet upon the Persian tongue.

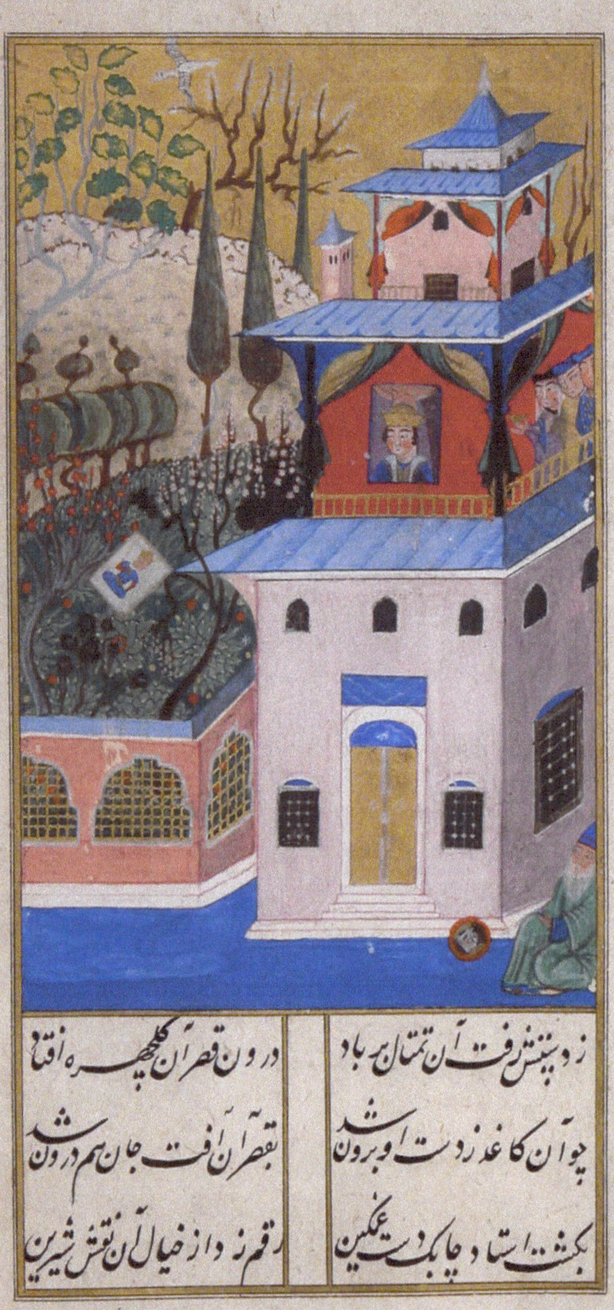
ز دستش رفت آن تمثال بر باد
درون قصر آن گلچهره افتاد
چو آن کاغذ ز دست او برون شد
بقصر آن آفت جان هم درون شد
بگشت استاد چابک دست غمگین
رقم زد از خیال آن نقش شیرین

This miniature style illustration in Page 23 depicts the scene: Shirin sees Khosrow's picture. There is two bottom panels of story in poetry, translated in a literary style:

Left Column:

The sight of your splendor set the soul aflame;
At that moment the picture slipped from his hand.
Wonder filled the place—
and every eye grew newly awakened.

Right Column:

Within the palace appeared a face like the horizon,
The painted image of that heart-ensnaring beauty.
The vision of that sweet enchantress
Pierced deep into the realm of imagination.

چو شد پرداخته آن صورت از نو — برسم تحفه بردش سوی خسرو

فتاد آن کاغذ تصویر ناگاه — بدست آن پری در گذرگاه

چو بر کاغذ نظر انداخت شیرین — بساطی دید چون بتخانهٔ چین

در آن مجلس دو صورت دید زیبا — که شد از مهر ایشان ناشکیبا

یکی او بود چون نیکو نظر کرد — ز مهر آن دگر یک دیده تر کرد

دل از شیرین ربود آن نقش دلکش — شد آن آشوب جهان زو مشوش

گرفت آن نقش از مهر در دست — نظر از غیر آن تمثال بربست

بزاری گفت ای نقش از کجایی — نمودار کدامین دلربایی

نمی دانم که نامت از که پرسم — ره جا و مقامت از که پرسم

بگو با من بلای جان من کیست — ندانم چون کنم درمان من چیست

مرا در یک نظر دیوانه کردی — ز خویش و آشنا بیگانه کردی

بسی بر گریها خندیده بودم — ز دوران درد و غم کم دیده بودم

باخر آنچه کردم پیشم آمد — ز محنت بر جگر صد نیشم آمد

Page 25 is the continuation of the illustrated page and scene: Shirin sees Khosrow. There is two panels of story in poetry, translated in a literary style:

Right Column:
When Khosrow's likeness came before her sight,
a marvel—sudden as lightning—filled the page.
She gazed upon the palace scene,
and there his form shone out
like the finest painting of China.
One instant he seemed alive before her,
the next—only a vision stirring the blood of her gaze.
Yet such sweetness flowed from that face
that her heart fled its dwelling.
"What name shall I give this stranger?" she wondered.
"From what realm has such beauty come?"
Like the scent of a rose-garden
his presence drew the soul from her breast.
She stood there—
half smiling,
caught in the dark coils of those painted curls—
and in that snare
her heart was taken captive.

Left Column:
Then she spoke:
"O companion of fortune,
why have you shown me this face?
Why cast such a snare before my
eyes?
With the chain of those curls
you have bound my heart.
My soul has gone after that
image,
and patience has fled my breast.
I no longer know myself—
reason has left me wandering.
If that moon-bright youth should
appear again,
perhaps my wounded heart might
heal.
But if he is only a painted dream,
then grief shall be my companion
—
for from that image
love has been born in me."

برآمد بانگ کوس و ناله نای ‌ ‌ دو کوه آهنین جنبند از جای
برون آمد هزاران آهنین تن ‌ ‌ نهان گردید چون آتش در آهن
ز دنداورنگ شه بر کوهه پیل ‌ ‌ یلان بستند صفها میل در میل
مهندس پیشکان چرخ پیمای ‌ ‌ ستاده برکف اسطرلاب بر جای
وزان جانب صف بهرام سرکش ‌ ‌ روان گردید چون دریای آتش
چو شد قلب و جناح هر دو صف راست ‌ ‌ فغان کرنای و کوس برخاست
ز هر جانب علم زد آتش کین ‌ ‌ دو لشکر را علمها گشت زرین
ز بانگ نای حتی مرد از جای ‌ ‌ در افتادی ز هولش بار از پای
جنیبتهای شیران قوی چنگ ‌ ‌ شده رقاص ز آواز ره جنگ
دو لشکر چون دو دریا ریخت بر هم ‌ ‌ هزاران کینه جو آویخت در هم
سپر گشته ترازوی بلا سنج ‌ ‌ همی پیمود بر شیر افکنان رنج
ز هر سو رشتهای عمر شیران ‌ ‌ بریده تیغ بر آن دلیران
هزاران تیرهای ناوک نیی ‌ ‌ چو نی لشکر همی خوردی پیاپی

Page 28 is the continuation of the illustrated page and scene: Shirin sees Khosrow. There is two panels of story in poetry, translated in a literary style, possibly from Shirin's perspective:

Right Column:
The cry rose out among the mountain heights,
And countless thoughts were left behind.
Doors and wounds and colors flared —
All twisting in their tangled coils.
At that sound the ranks drew up,
Strong as a single mighty hand.
From every side bright banners blazed,
And every trumpet-call rang clear.
Forces surged like the sea in motion,
Companions clung together fast.
More shattered than crown or broken reed,
His loosened curls fell down.
And the gaze sank deep
Into the mirror of the water.

Left Column:
With two bright seeing eyes
Show my image to the gaze.
Sit before the heart's pure light
And speak of the mountain-like king.
Let the eyes flow like burning water,
Cry aloud in that bright stillness.
Behold the banner of revelation raised,
Casting its burning radiance behind.
Within the heart a judge arose—
My heart decided in a single breath.
Who could equal such strength?
Whether fortune turned this way or that.
A bond was formed of itself,
A bond the heart had never known before.

تکاور رمان بزیر پیل زوران
گرو برده بگاه تک گوران

زمین در ماتم گردان کین جوی
زده ناخن زنقش نعل بر روی

چو بد مهران کمانهای کیانی
زطاق ابروان جان ستانی

زهر سو گشته خنجرهای خونریز
بخوان چون غمزه کافردلان تیز

خدنگ شیر مردان سینه جسته
زقتل سرکشان در خون نشسته

دوان پیک اجل هر سوی چون تیر
که گردد جنگ گیر از عنان گیر

فراز کشتگان تیر و خنجر
درفش کاویای سایه گستر

غریو نعره شیران شرزه
درین پیکار افکنده لرزه

زره چشم خون پالا زحد بیش
که خون گرید بمرگ صاحب خویش

کلاه خود یلان زهر آشام
زبهر شربت مرگ آمده جام

پی اماج گاه تیر کینه
شده صندوقها صندوق سینه

بآخر خسرو از سرپنجه کین
شکست آور بر بهرام چوبین

گرفت آن گرد گردنکش ره خویش
نزارا داغ حسرت بر دل ریش

Page 31 is still the continuation of the illustrated page and scene: Shirin sees Khosrow. There is two panels of story in poetry, translated in a literary style:

Right Column:
So slender there it seemed—
narrower even than a strand of hair
—
My fragile waist bound in that girdle.
As when two lovers meet in an embrace,
Sweet words entwined with sweetness.
The laughter of lion-hearted men rose like a clear spring;
Two among them lifted cups of wine.
A vow was sworn upon that glance—
Dark and radiant together—
and before my eyes
Wings seemed suddenly to appear.
In that instant when the vision came,
The heart itself was seized.

Left Column:

If one were to pass that place
and cast but a single glance,
speech itself would fly from the
village,
so wondrous was that sight.
The tale of that sweet, intoxicated
beauty
spread among hearts,
binding breath to breath
in hidden knots of love.
Carpets were spread beneath the
shade,
and the valley among the stones
looked on.
With a single greeting
joy rose for the fortunate one.
Though time and death bring
harshness,
and hardship walks beside fate,
Yet at the fountain's head
that sorrow was broken.

کمانها از قوی زوران مشوش	فتا در کشاکشهای ناخوش
کشیدی جنگجویان سپهدار	بروی آشتی از تیغ دیوار
ز چاکاچاک خنجر سینه‌ها چاک	شده دلها بمرگ از زندگیها پاک

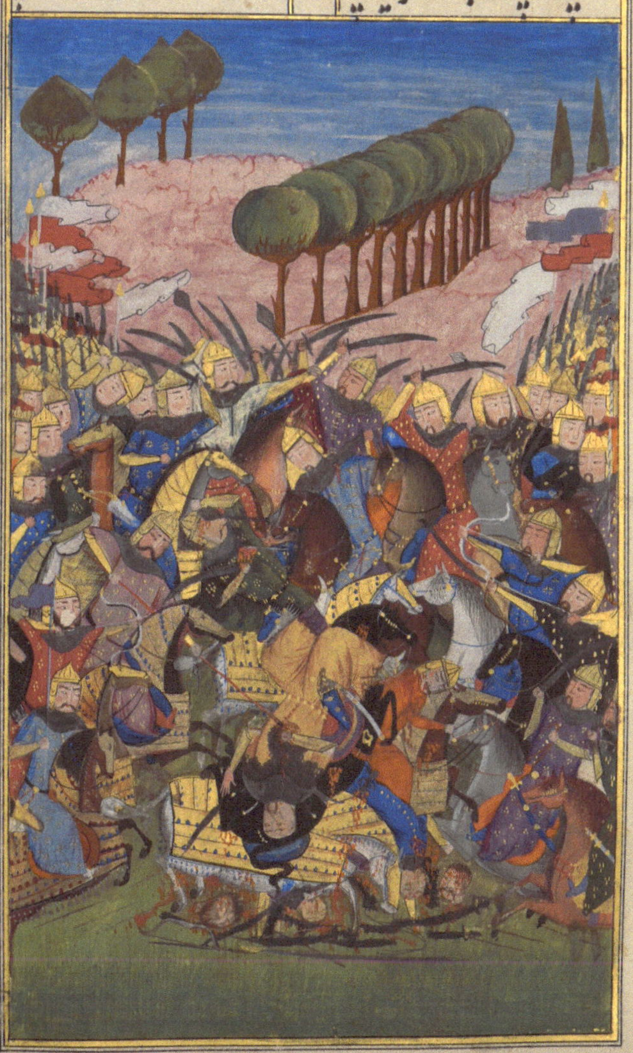

After Khosrow and Shirin merged their hearts, page 34 depicts a battle scene in the narrative surrounding Khosrow. After his father dies, he loses a battle to rebel general named Bahram Chobin. Khosrow then flees to Byzantine Empire and is forced to marry the Emperor's daughter, Maryam, in exchange for an army to win back his throne in a second battle with Bahram Chobin.

Right Column:
Fate brought ruin upon them,
and battle was drawn with flashing
Indian blades.
From the dust of the earth
Blood scattered everywhere.

Left Column:
Behind them the struggle raged fiercely
—
On the battlefield beneath the Roman
swords
Warriors in golden armor
were struck down.

نهم که لاله را بر سینه داغی / گهی گل را بر افروزم چراغی

گهی از گل بر آرم خان را خار / زمانی کوه را بر دل نهم بار

کنم از نرگس مستانهٔ خویش / غزالانرا پیک دیوانهٔ خویش

سحاب رحمت آمد جانب کوه / گیاه تشنه رست از درد و اندوه

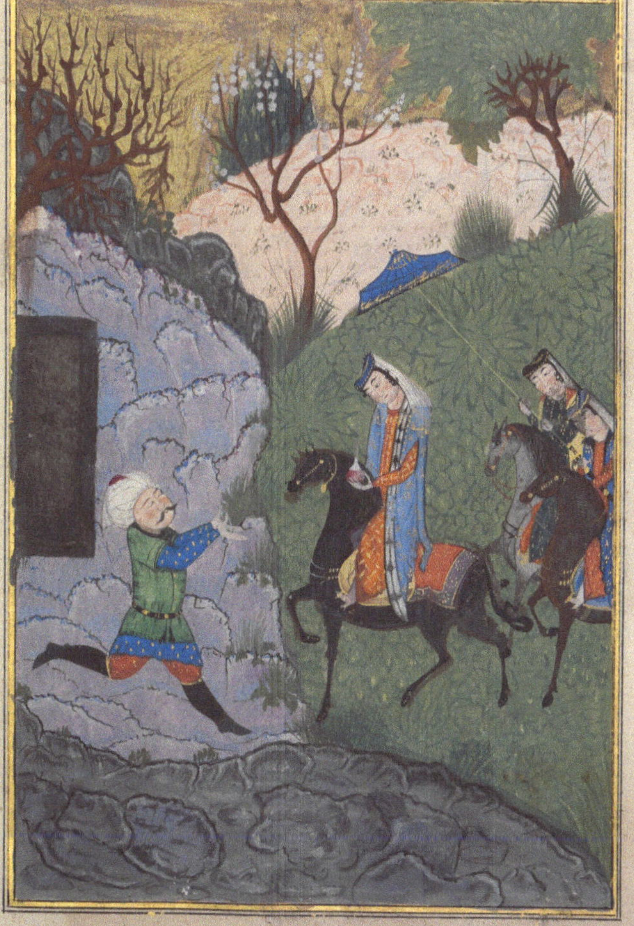

The miniature on page 36 shows a period where Khosrow disappeared for a long time, and was thought lost or dead. In the countryside, Shirin sees Farhat, a talented sculptor. Farhat immediately falls for Shirin and gives her flowers. His love is reciprocated. Later in the story, Farhat will attempt to carve a massive channel in the mountain to bring Shirin fresh milk. The short columns show the flame of love, possibly told from Farhat's side.

Right Column:
I set the tulip of longing upon my breast
as if it were a cure—
yet in that instant
it rends the careless heart.
I praise the sweetness of your dark tresses,
like rain clouds drifting
over the trees of the mountain.

Left Column:
Whoever bears such wounds of flame
must cry from the mountain of sorrow.
Gazelles mirror your form and grace,
and memory of you
holds twin griefs within the heart.

همه شکرلب و شیرین تبسم   همه غنچه دهان و خوش تکلم

بیکجا جمع گشته آفتی چند   سرو سرخیل شیرین شکرخند

گشاده نرگس مست از سر ناز   کسی کم دیده با دام دهن باز

کشیده بر رخ زیبا خط نیل   که باشد از پی چشم بدان میل

گرفته زاغ زلفش بر صنوبر   ز در گوشوارش بیضه در بر

دهانش را لب نوشین می ناب   باب زندگی پرورده عناب

بگرد مه ز معجر هاله بسته   شب قدرش نهفته در کلاله

سر انداز آمدش صبح و رخش روز   زهی آن صبح روز عالم افروز

بیا را گفت آن شیرین شمایل   بسوی بیستونم میکشد دل

سحاب بیستون خواهم شد امروز   که بینم برق آه آن جگر سوز

چو تیشش کند در جان شکار   بود کاندر دل سنگم کند کار

زنم در بیستون از نازکامی   بکبک کوه آموزم خرامی

ریاحین را کنم در جلوه پامال   زمین را ماه گون بخشم بخلخال

Page 38 continues on the emotional turmoil between Shirin and Farhad, possibly told from Farhad's perspective:

Right Panel:
My head was filled
With the sweetness of those lips;
A gathering of companions formed.
The order of things shifted again,
and a line was drawn upon that
beautiful face.
His raven hair made captives of hearts,
While wisdom flowed from his honeyed
mouth.
He spoke—yet hid the meaning in his
breast,
And tears fell from the secret within.
Bring the reed of indigo color;
From him sorrow mingled with
reproach.
He himself became the coin of the
world,
Soft in the palm of destiny,
Stretching long within the midst of fate.

Left Column:

Whatever I once was—life and joy—
My will and spirit were shattered.
I said: the eye itself
is caught like prey within me,
As sweetness rises like sugar from the reed.
His soul was seized
like a moth drawn to the flame.
The night of his fortune was crowned,
and morning lit the days.
Within the hidden heart
the scent of paradise appeared,
Yet his lightning
burned the liver with longing.
Perhaps I too
have become another sinner,
learning the tumult of love's battle,
While on this earth
my path lies wandering in dreams.

همایون لطف آن خورشید سایه | بران بوم خراب افگند سایه

چو آن فریادرس را دید فرهاد | دویدش پیش و کرد از درد فریاد

فتاد از شوق در پای سمندش | که گردد خاک سرو سربلندش

زبان عذر بگشاد از سر سوز | که ای طلعت شب هجرم را روز

شدی در کوه جانم را تسلی | تعالی الله زهی طور تجلی

من جان داده را زین دلنوازی | ز نو جان دادی و جان را درازی

پی نظاره‌ات ای غیرت حور | مرا چشم آمدی و چشم را نور

خجل شد زین سبب خصم سیه دل | بماندش از خجالت پای در گل

درونی شاد و بیرونی خجل ماند | نه چاک پیرهن نه چاک دل ماند

رخ از برق نمودی ای پری چهر | شبم را صبح دادی صبح را مهر

دل از من صبر من از من داشت دوری | مرا دل دادی و دل را صبوری

دل ریش از تو امید وفا داشت | جراحت مرهم و مرهم دوا داشت

من خاکی که گرد آستانم | رساندی ز آستان بر آسمانم

The panel on page 41 continues to describe the mutual affect and longing between Shirin and Farhat, possibly from Shirin's perspective

Right Column:

The shadow of your kindness reached my soul;
I saw my beloved burning like a moving flame.
My drunken feet stumbled into longing,
and its color never left my mind.
A jewel-like spirit, a cup of comfort—
yet my life was given away
to its burden.
At times the heart lay like a bed upon the earth;
at times two visions appeared,
while sleep and wine drifted together.
But the soil of the heart
could not bear such softness—
for before you even loyalty could not endure.
Love itself rose like grass from the ground.

Left Column:

Thus I blossomed like a flower in spring,
as gifts were brought again.
My head and heart were poured out together;
the fire of night became my lamp.
Loneliness lengthened its road,
and from the soul
a new cry of lament arose.
Yesterday joy filled my eyes,
yet the scent of flowers bound me like chains.
The tears of the beloved split the eye with pain—
and I cannot surrender
either the morning or the treasure of my heart.
At first patience was granted,
but the wound of sorrow deepened;
and no one knew the grief I carried.

After Farhat and Shirin's love blossoms, Khosrow comes back to Persia to reclaim his kingdom and soon he loses his wife Maryam. Jealous of Farhad, sends a messenger to the sculptor with false news that Shirin has died. Overcome with grief, Farhad strikes his head against the rocks and dies instantly. Shirin is devastated and furious at Khosrow's cruelty. After some time, Khosrow manages to reclaim Shirin's heart. The following parts will tell the story of their renewed love, followed by a scene of countryside celebration.

زآتشناک رویان پرازرم / شده هنگامهای دلبری گرم

رسانیدش سروسرخیل اعصر / بجشنهای شاهی تا در قصر

بقصر آمد درون زیبا سرشتی / قدم زد حورزادی بهشتی

نشست آن شاه گیتی خرم و شاد / بمی خوردن صلای خسروی داد

حریفان ساغر می برگرفتند / نشاط و خوشدلی از سر گرفتند

گل افشاندند و می در جام کردند / عذار ساقیان گلفام کردند

برآمد نالهٔ چنگ و چغانه / ز نغمهای مطرب شد ترانه

پری پیکر درون حجلهٔ ناز / بگردش صف زده خوبان طناز

سراسر غنچهای ناشکفته / همه در پردهٔ عصمت نهفته

رسیده لالها هر یک ز باغی / نه لاله بلکه هر یک شب چراغی

یکی از تکمهٔ دیپای زردوز / پر از میوه نهال خاطرافروز

یکی را مشتری آویزهٔ گوش / یکی را اطلس گردون سراغوش

یکی فرخ همای نازنینی / ز هر سو گشته بالش آستینی

Right Column:

From narrowness
I drew speech into the open—
an excuse
Like violet and lily in bloom.
You heard the tale
within the turning world,
Where good companions
sat together in fortunate accord.
From the unseen
a single secret rose—
A fairy-formed beauty
veiled in radiance.
Suddenly a face appeared with prayer,
A tulip-colored steed
entering the garden.
One pillar
from two hidden roots—
A blessed essence
within creation.

Left Column:
The leaves grew restless
with the noise of gathering.
His glance moved lightly,
even to the smallest finger.
He lowered himself from his saddle,
while the cry of festivity rose.
Joy returned
and hearts grew bright again.
From the world he gathered
strength
And assembled the circle of
dervishes.
All sat
behind the veil of purity.
From the tulip-hued mount
a light appeared—
And whoever sees this tale
may wander, astonished.

بشکر خنده شیرین شکرخند — شکسته قدر شکر قیمت قند

بدین آیین نگار نازپرور — نشسته بر بتان دست سرور

درآمد شهریار از باده سرمست — بت طناز را بنشاند و بنشست

بساط خسروی جام جمشید — در آن منزل قران ماه و خورشید

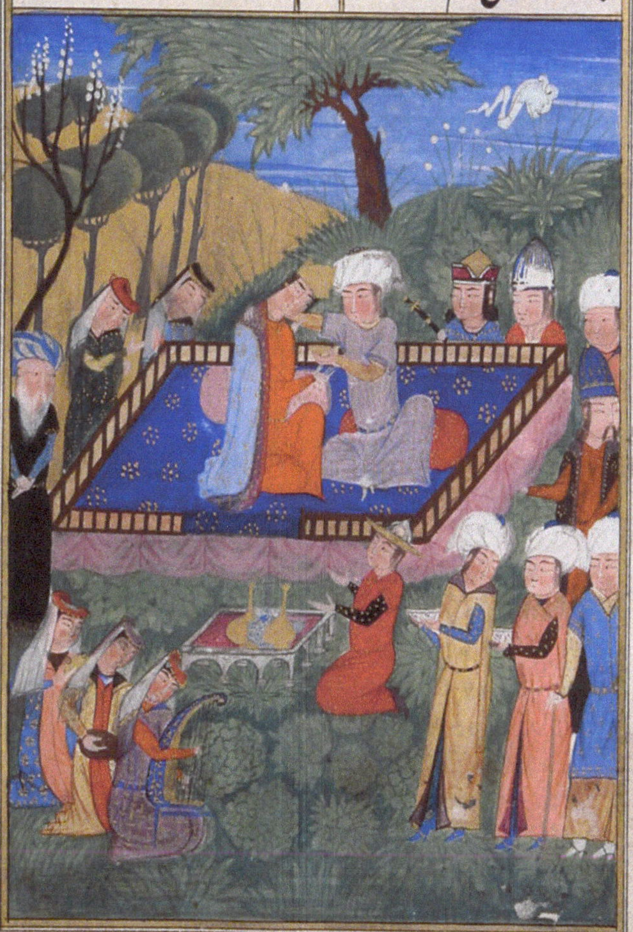

The miniature on Page 48 depicts the later phases of the story, where Khusrow and Shirin are back together in the countryside, enjoying a celebration on their honor.

Right Panel

The idol of beauty
touches sweet music with her fingertips;
and men lay their noble heads at her feet.
Into the fire of every sorrow
they entrust their secrets to her
—
for wisdom and life alike have tasted that flame.

Left Panel

Before destiny
truth falls like minted gold.
A willow bends beside his lips.
The idol-hearted soul
does not rush into the fire—
there, in that resting place, it finds its peace.

نشسته بر مراد خویش داور / شده معشوقه یار و بخت یاور

بدست آن زلف عنبرفام بودش / عجب ماری بافسون رام بودش

گهی دادی ز بوسه داد دل را / گرفتی در بر آن ماه چگل را

بشیرین شاه را شد اشتها تیز / که بود آن شهد نوش رغبت انگیز

ندیدان شب صلاح کار شیرین / که بردارد ز درجش مهر دیرین

ز بهر آنکه خسرو بود بیهوش / شدی در سفتنش فردا فراموش

خورد چون پسته را مست سرانداز / نداند بسته لب را از دهن باز

بگاه خواب ماه فتنه انگیز / برون آمد دمی از پیش پرویز

زنیمرادان آن شوخ شکرخند / بدو سیمین عذاری بود مانند

در و پوشید یکسر زیور خویش / فرستادش بسوی دلبر خویش

شهنشه بود از می مست بی تاب / یکی در پیش او شهتوت و عناب

بعنابی روان شهتوت را خورد / نشد فهمش که آن سافت و یا درد

سحر که خواب مستی چشم بگشاد / سخن پرسید از آن شوخ پری زاد

Right Column:
He sat there himself
upon the road of fate—
And the turning heavens
bent away and vanished.
Toward him, with heart and body,
Sweet-spirited Shirin
sat upright.
From her lips
no cry of pain arose;
Instead she spoke
of joy
and of kisses.
For the secret lies hidden
within the hand itself—
And the moon of sleep
grew faint.
That bright morning
smiled beside him,
Yet in his eyes
restlessness still wandered.
He sat there,
uneasy in heart,
Until at last
sleep carried him away—
For many lovers
are broken this way.

Left Column:
The moon's light rose again in belief;
A strange meaning
settled upon the night.
Had that sweet city
been foreign,
You might have taken
the moon of forty nights from me.
Those who were there came near;
They turned
and raised themselves again.
From the lips
came music and secret speech,
And the face
awakened in its own light.
Like a gazelle
he appeared to the eye,
Sending goodness
into his own soul.
He sat in prayer,
quiet and content—
until the hour returned.
And when I rise again
from this moment,
Perhaps no one will remember me.

شتر مرغ از کبوتر هم فزونست — که در پرواز باید دید چونست

مسلم نامه سنجی نظامی — تو باری نیستی زان نامه نامی

بجز بر دیگری نازو چنانست — که بر داماد نازد رایگانست

ز حسن شاهدان دلاله راچه — ز نور مشعل مه هاله راچه

نباشد چون ترا ناخن در انگشت — شوی عاجز چو ناگه خار در پشت

گهی گر تشنگی بی تاب گردی — بذکر دجله کی سیراب گردی

گرت زین جنس در بازار باشد — ترا هم مشتری بسیار باشد

دران فرصت که گشتم نقش پرداز — که این دیبای چینی را کنم ساز

هزاران بود نقش دلفریبم — که بردی هریکی از جان شکیبم

ازینها نقش بستم اندکی را — نکردم جلوه گر از صد یکی را

ز کار خویشتن دل سیر بودم — ازان صنعت گری کمتر نمودم

بمن گر داشتی کس اهتمامی — بدورش دیدی از هر کامی

نی کلکم دمیدی انچنان صور — که فردوسی بر آوردی سر از گور

Right Column:
Though the palace
was veiled in mystery,
the word itself
was meant for one listener.
Thus we receive it from him—
for within beauty
a hidden sign of the beloved
remains.
When the kingdom
rose in power,
it left even mountains
thirsting without water.
Yet the earth grew pleasant again,
and the sea returned—
while through the tale
the cry of lament was heard.
Thousands are named
in the story of love;
yet from this fragile life
I draw the thread tighter.
Where I carried away
the sweeter heart,
look well
at the words of those who spoke.
Even the willow
seems to send a messenger.

Left Column:
Behind the veil
we heard a voice—
and with careful attention
its secret could be known.
It touched the hem
like a wave upon the sea,
twisting like a tulip
from sweet lips.
Toward the lovers
the message moved,
forming in passing
a dark and circling ring.
The wounds of existence
are many—
and if I open
this gate of meaning,
my wandering dervish
will gather them together,
for breath itself
forms the circle of unity.
Yet little grows
within that ring—
and the lone wanderer
turns his face toward it.

نه پنداری این دعوی گزافست | بیان واقعست اینها نه لافست
گرت این نکته باور نیست چندان | بیا بسم الله اینک گوی و چوگان
اگر طبع ترا باشد شناسی | ازین هم می توان کردن قیاسی
بیا ای هاتفی این گفت و گو چند | زبان درکش لب از دعوی فروبند
سخن را ختم کردان بر دعایی | که این دعوی رسد هم خود بجایی
خداوندا چو این نادره بکر | برون آمد ز نخل نو بر فکر
چنانش کن ز خوبی شور بازار | که باشد مشتری از جان خریدار

به نیکویی چنان کن نامدارش
که باشد بر سعادت ختم کارش

شد تمام این کتاب ورجند | دلگشایی کند بغمخواره
فرح قلب حاصلست او را | هر که این اورد بنظاره
خط و تذهیب و تبر و تصویرش | شد ز دست من دل آواره
بیشتر زین چون توانم کرد | که مرا یک دلیست صد پاره
شد تمامی این دما تاریخ

Right Column:
Do not imagine
that this claim I speak
is merely words
raising dust in the air.
If your nature
knows how to recognize truth,
then tell me—
what piety stands between us
now?
Let speech be sealed
with prayer.
Call upon the name
and the command of the Lord
—
and you will see
prosperity return to the world.

Left Column:
The explanation came
and quietly departed.
Even the name of God
must sometimes be spoken softly.
From a little sign
one may judge much—
between those who claim
and those who truly know.
For a claim
that leaves the path of reason
turns only
into astonishment before the
beloved

Middle Rubric:
Remember the Lord
with goodness—
for a single breath
in eternity
is already
its completion.

This book
has reached its end.
May a fortunate heart
receive its reward.
Written in tale
and woven in verse—
what more ending
could be desired?
May someone open it
without need or pride,
and read its name.
For the author
held only one thing:
a heart
bound to the beloved.

Summary and storyline of Khosrow and Shirin varies by authors, eras, cultural influence, and different lands where it is told. General story pattern includes the main character Khosrow. a fictionalized version of the historical Sasanian King Khosrow II (r. 590–628 AD), portrayed as a passionate, complex, and often mercurial lover. He is a Persian ruler who falls in love with the Armenian princess Shirin, navigating exile, war, and intense romantic rivalry with a sculptor named Farhad.

This specific manuscript is notable for being produced by a single individual compared to typical patter of the time, where inscriptions by multiple calligraphers and illustrators work on one piece. Calligraphy, illumination, and all paintings were completed by an artist named Suzi (meaning "the burning one").

The entire sheet measures approximately 24 cm (H) x 16.4 cm (W) (9 7/16 x 6 7/16 inches).
Materials: Created using ink, opaque watercolor, and gold on paper, with a traditional leather binding.
Illustrations: It contains seven paintings executed in a style that bridges western Iranian (Aq Quyunlu) traditions with emerging Ottoman and European influences.

Calligraphy Style: The text is written in nasta'liq script, the standard for Persian romantic epics.

Decorative Elements:
Double Frontispiece: The opening pages resemble luxury Qur'ans of the period but are slightly less elaborate.

Illumination: Includes gold-filled bands with medallions containing verses of text.

Realism: Unlike traditional Persian "idealized" art, this manuscript uses early shadowing and perspective, particularly in architectural details like palace balconies and iron grilles.

Provenance & Origin

Date: Completed in 904 AH (1498–99 CE).

Geography: Attributed to Turkey, likely produced in Istanbul or Amasya during the reign of Ottoman Sultan Bayezid II.

Significance: It serves as a key artifact demonstrating how Persian literature was adapted and celebrated within the Ottoman court. Additional information can be found in Metropolitan Museum of Art's webpage, which also publishes the raw copies of some pages. https://www.metmuseum.org/art/collection/search/452037

Perennifolio Press proudly presents a collectible copy of the story pages from the published public domain pages, found in the Metropolitan Art Museum. Our editors reformatted pages to create aesthetic experience, designed a new classical format to put the available pages back in the order of the story line. The last pages of the book were left blank intentionally to allow journaling and notes. We wish you a pleasant reading and art experience.

Commentary

Khosrow and Shirin is an epic romance originated from Persia, then spread to much of Middle East and Mediterranean. The story is built on the real life of Persian King Khosrow and Armenian Princess Shirin who lived in 6th century AD. Over the centuries, multiple iterations were told in the vast lands and the story was retold in many generations. Themes of jealousy, immaturity, pain, loyalty, piety, love and passion, as well as communication, diplomacy, serendipity play out in the story entangled with the three main characters. Nizami Ganjavi, a 12th century poet created a most beloved and complex version of the story. In this version Shirin is viewed as the most beloved character surpassing the influence of Khosrow, an independent, strong, educated, and loving propagandist. Below are links for the expanded story and analysis based on the story. This manuscript follows much shorter version by Hatifi in 15th century with Ottoman flair.

Bibliography

https://www.ijss-sn.com/uploads/2/0/1/5/20153321/mohamad_esfehani_paper_05_-_june_2017.pdf

https://www.peopleofar.com/2015/11/08/before-romeo-and-juliet-there-was-khosrow-and-shirin/

https://ia601808.us.archive.org/16/items/khosrow-shirin/Khosrow_Shirin.pdf

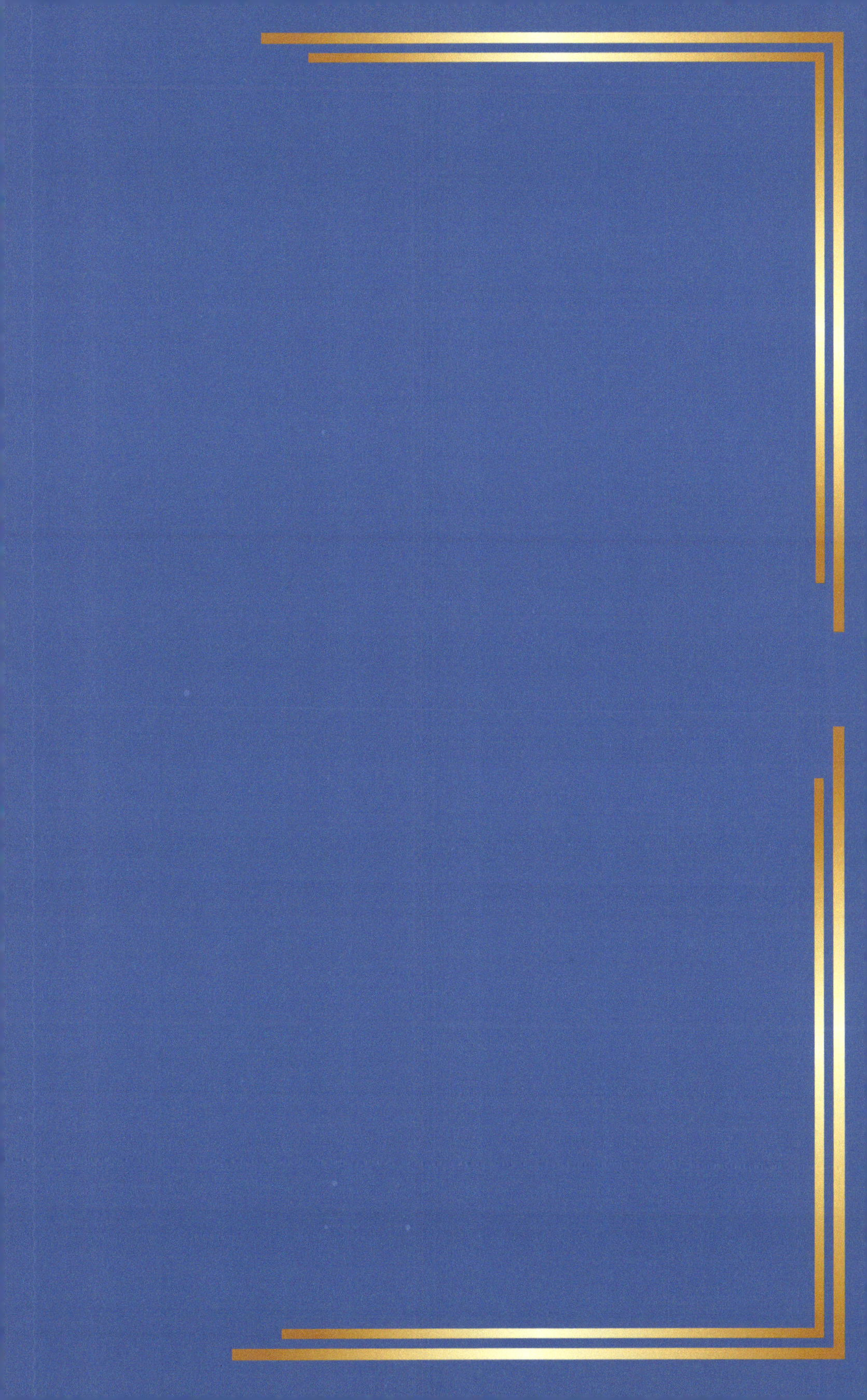

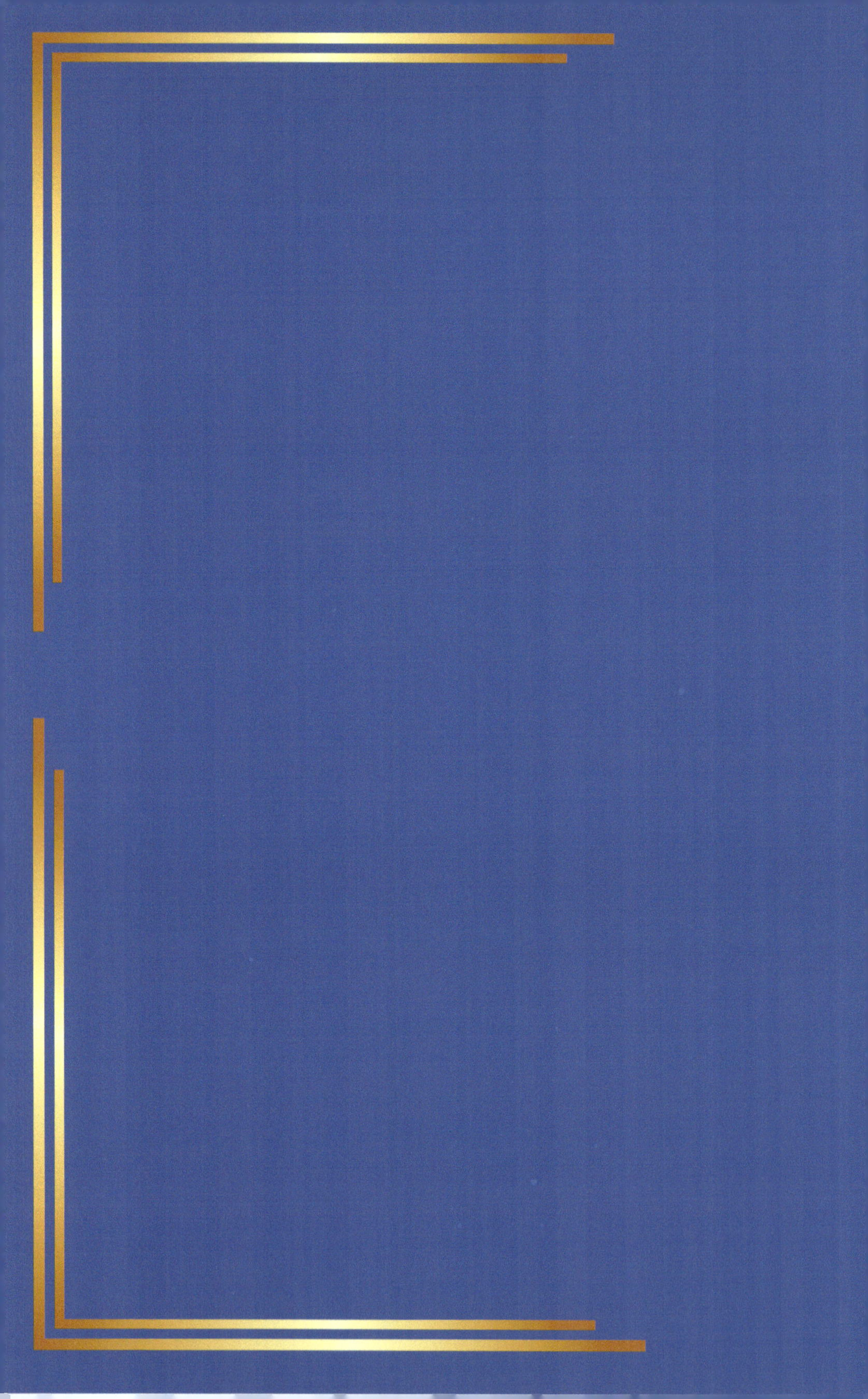

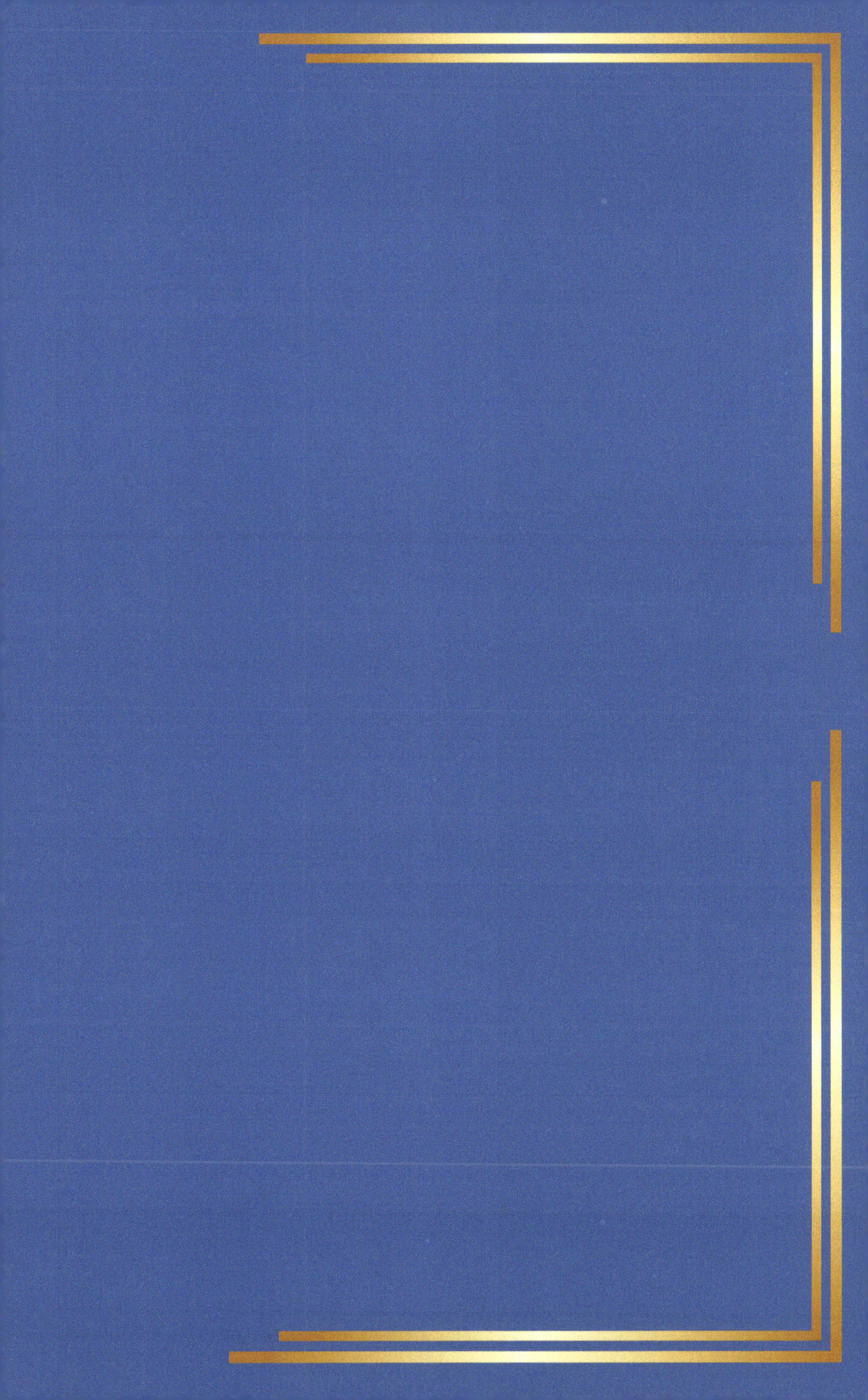

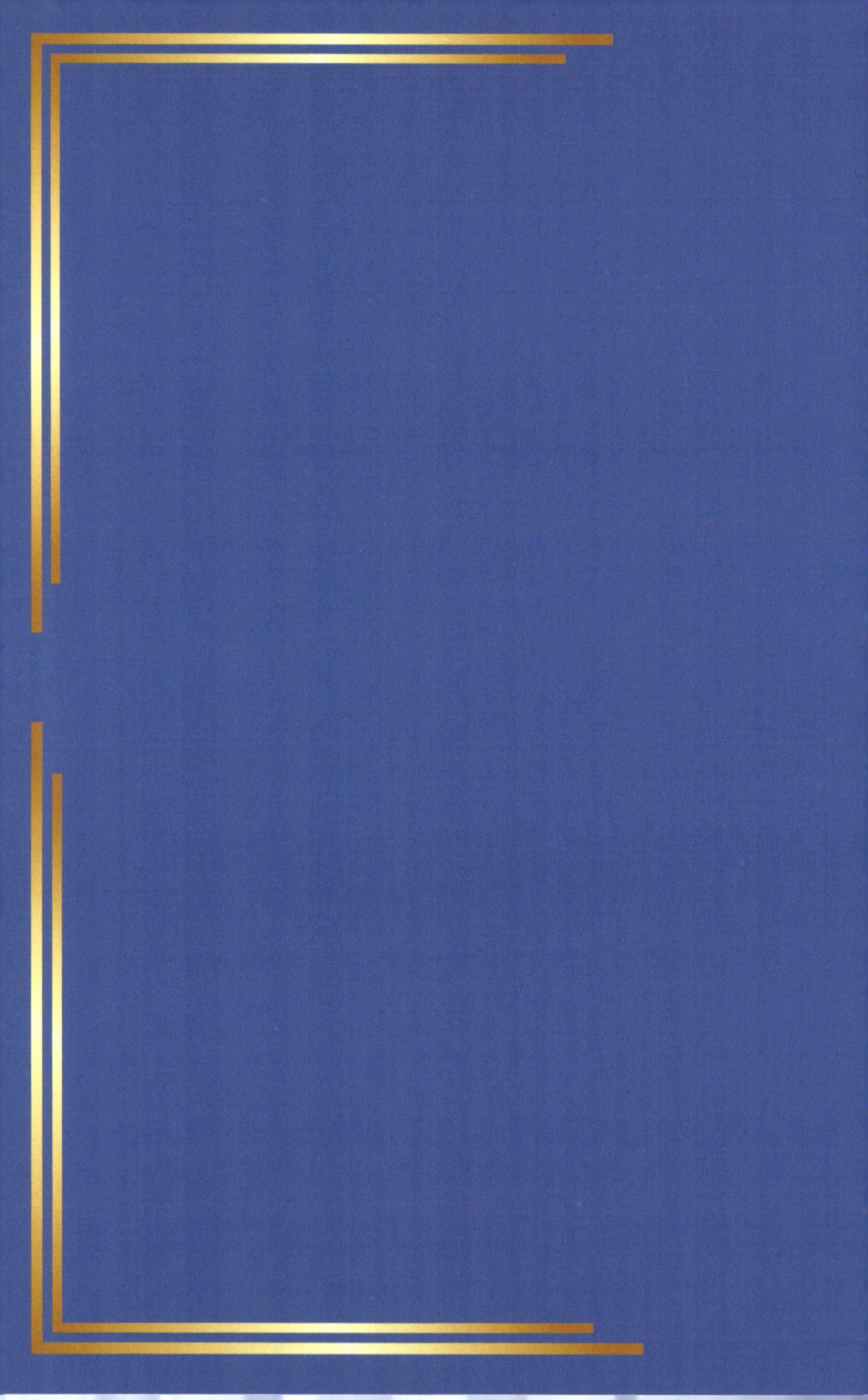

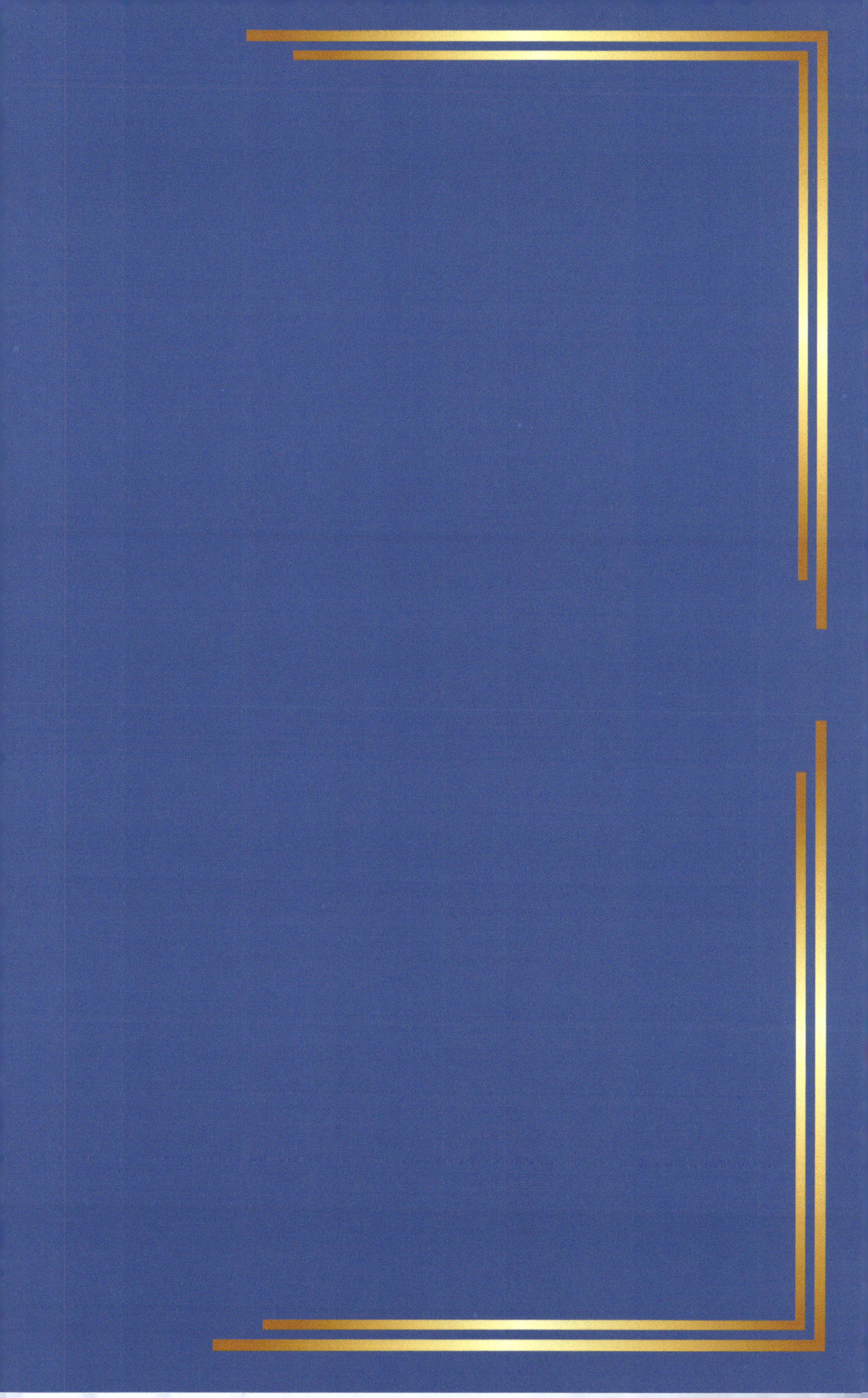

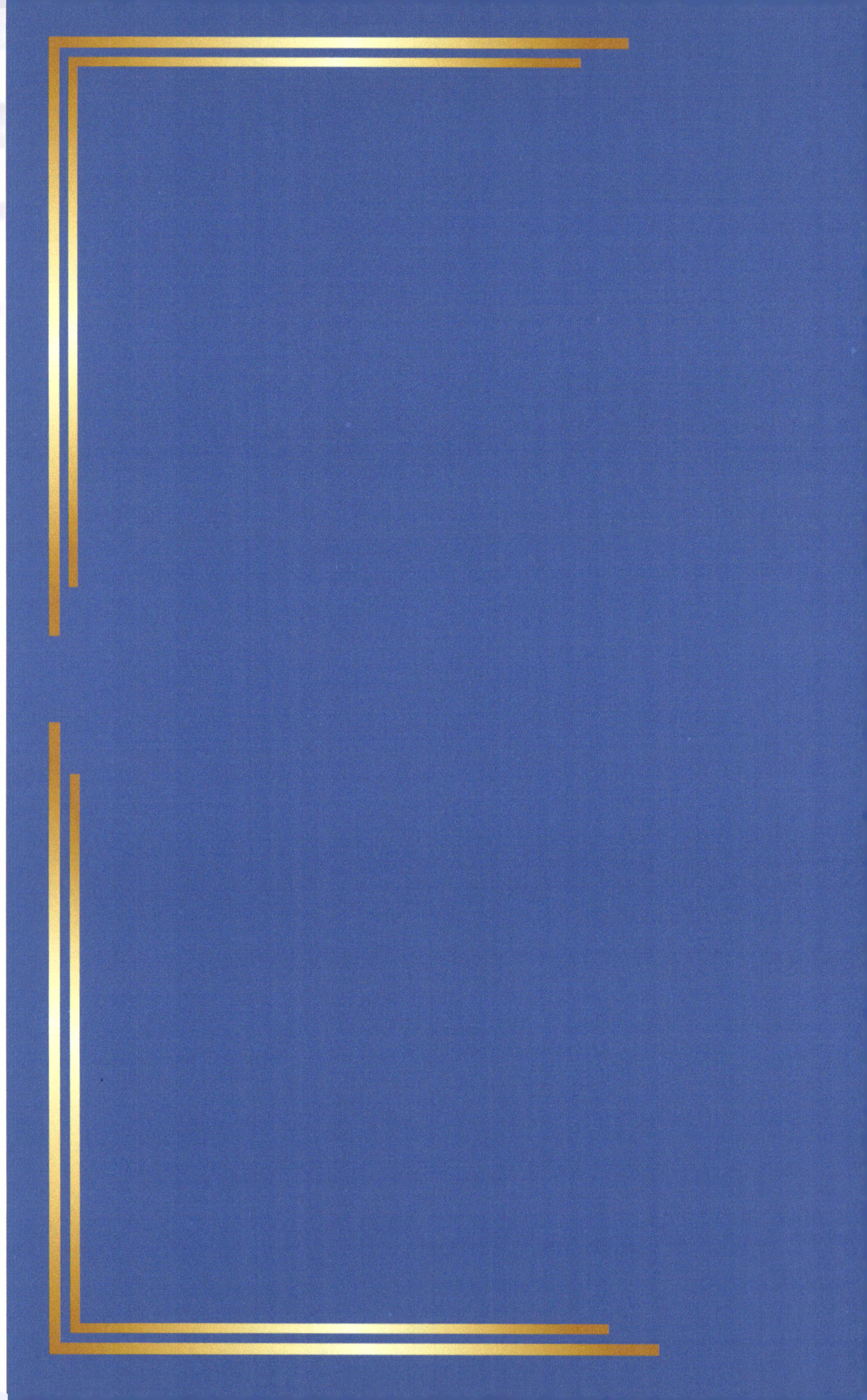

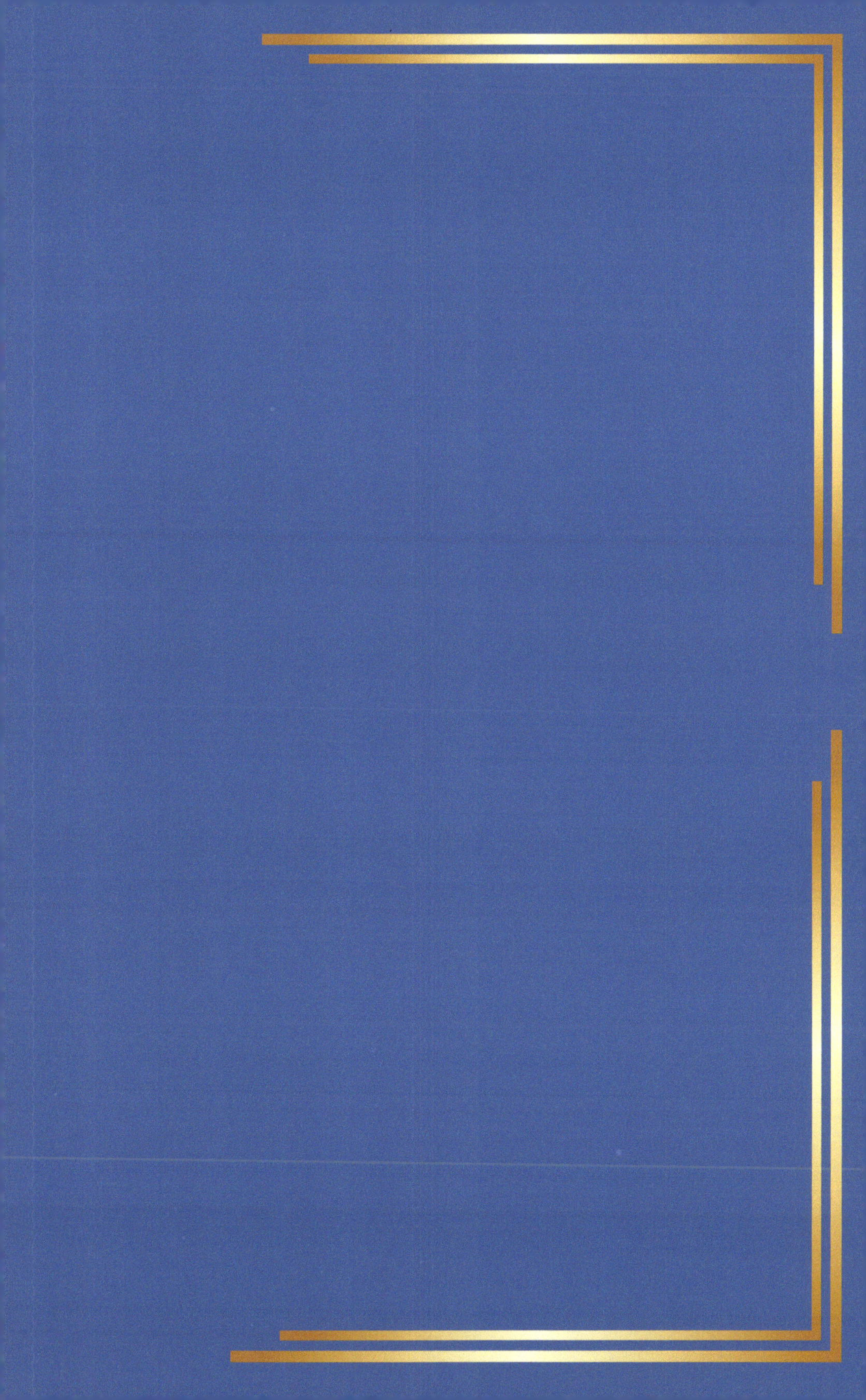

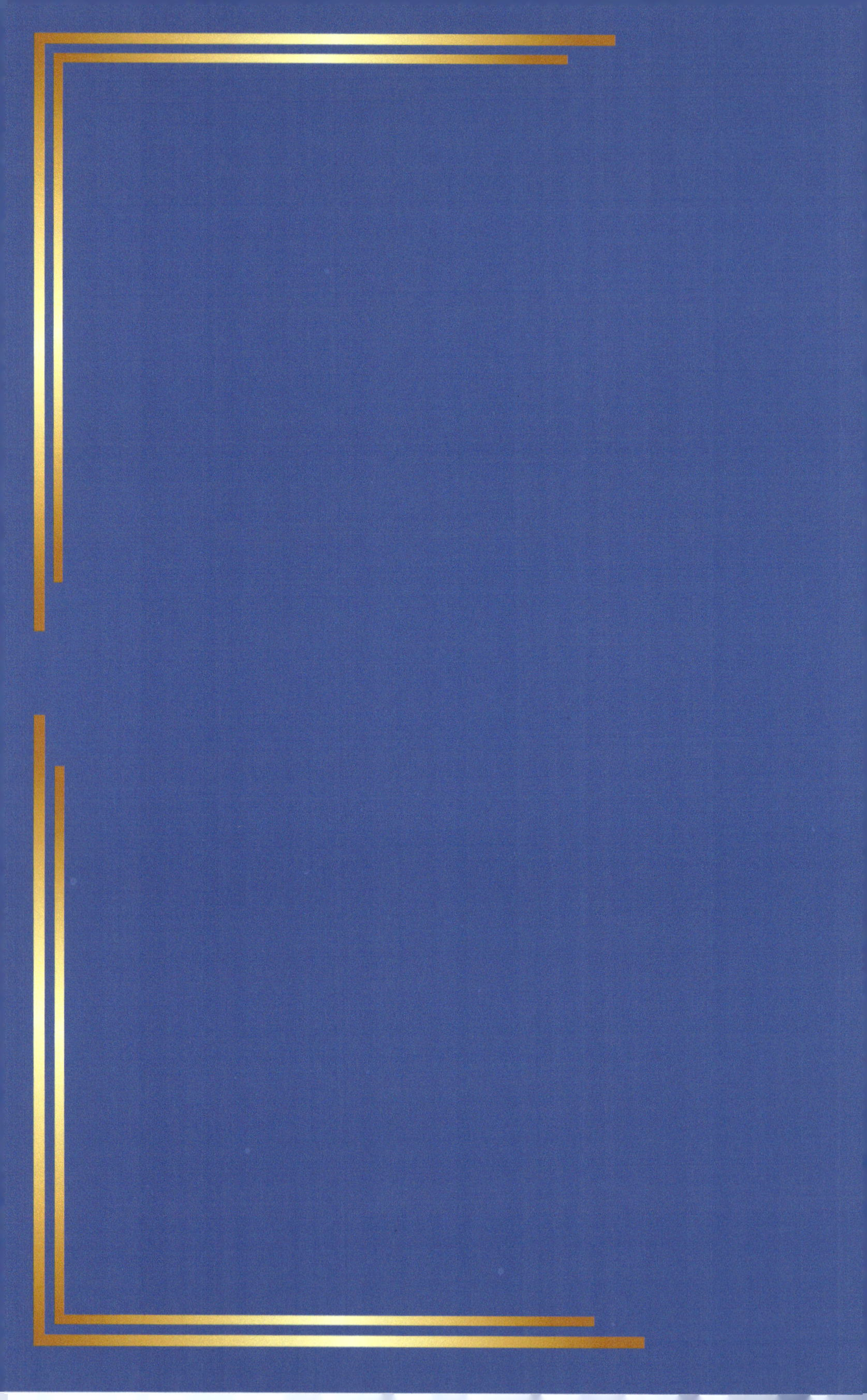

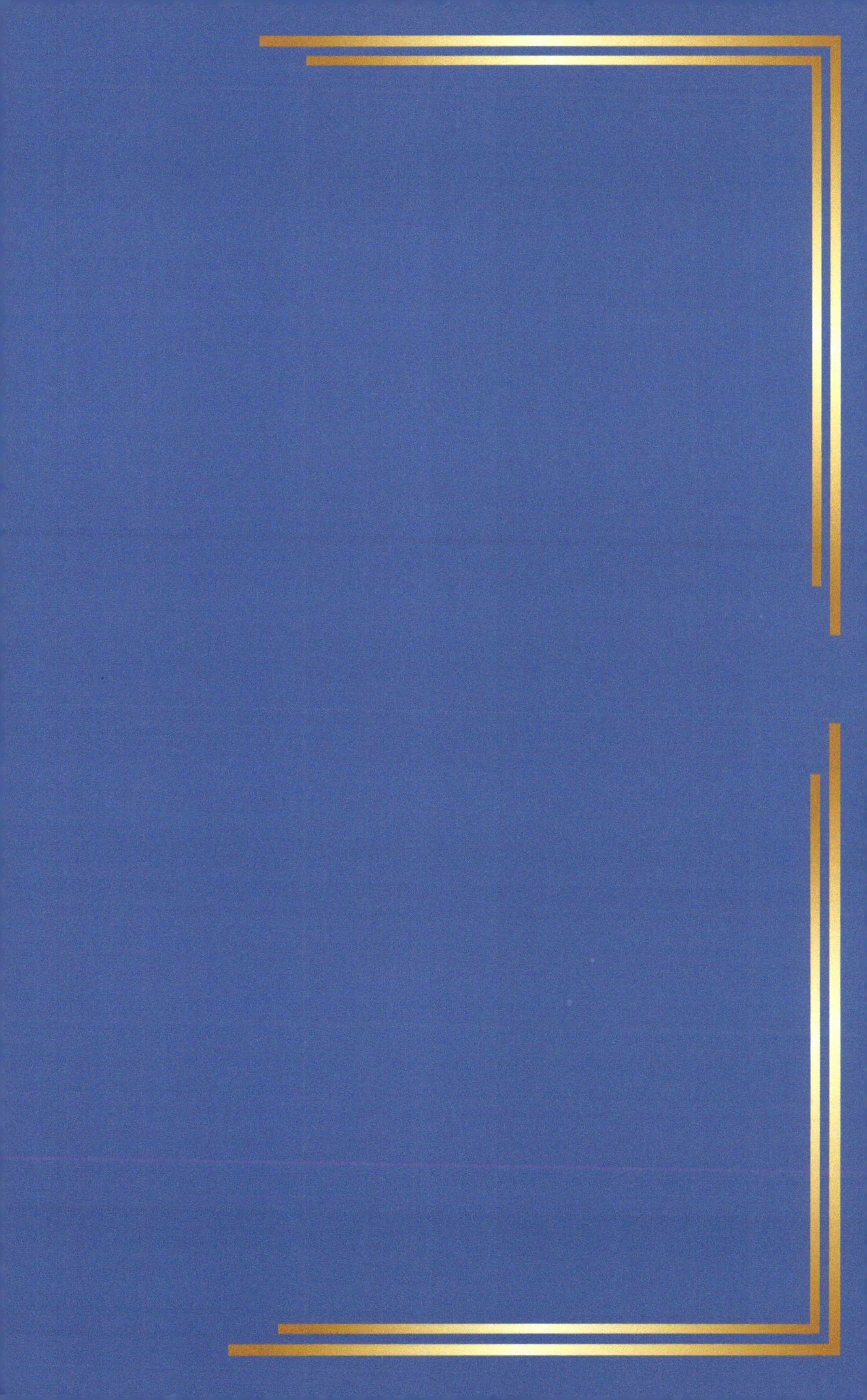

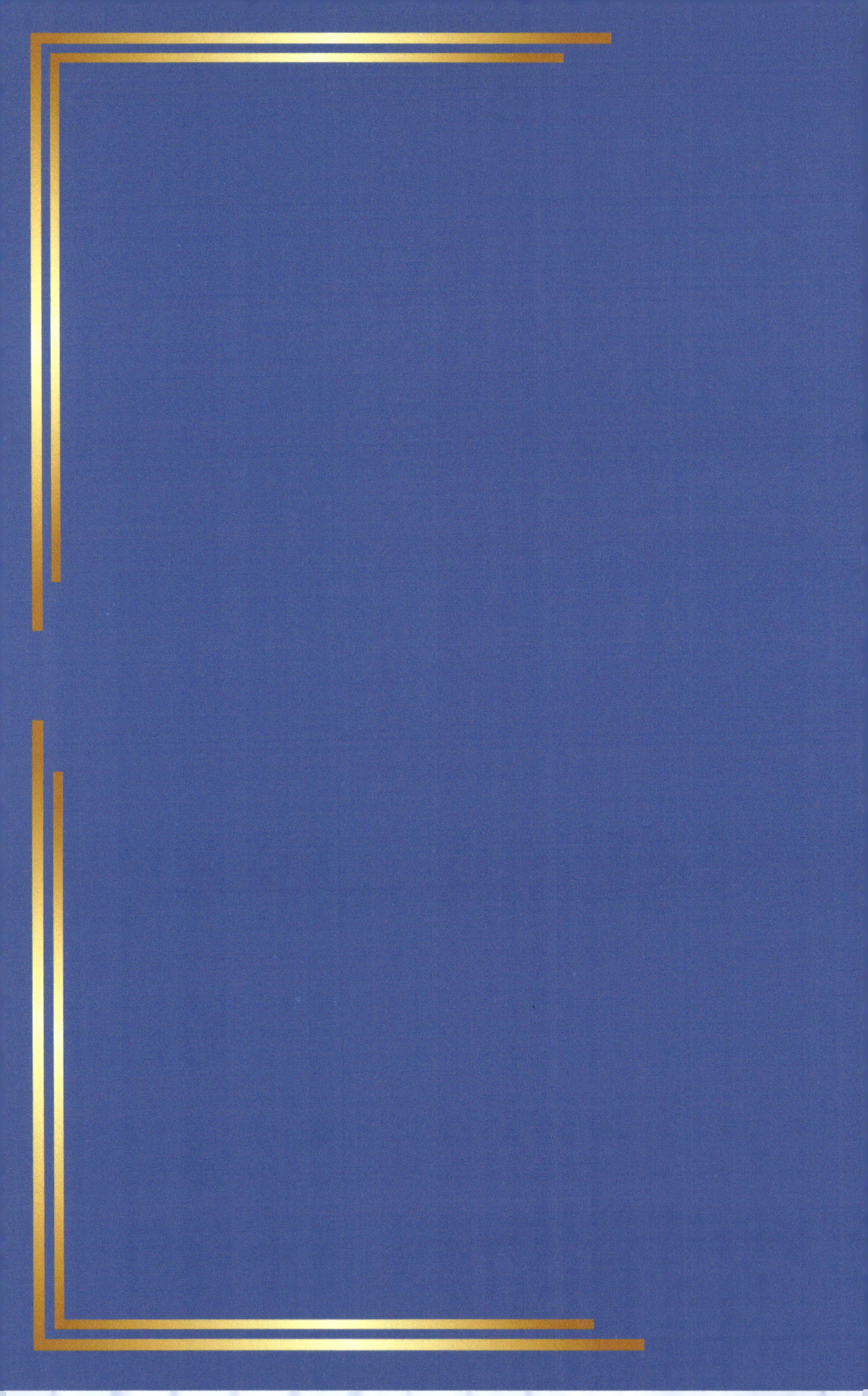

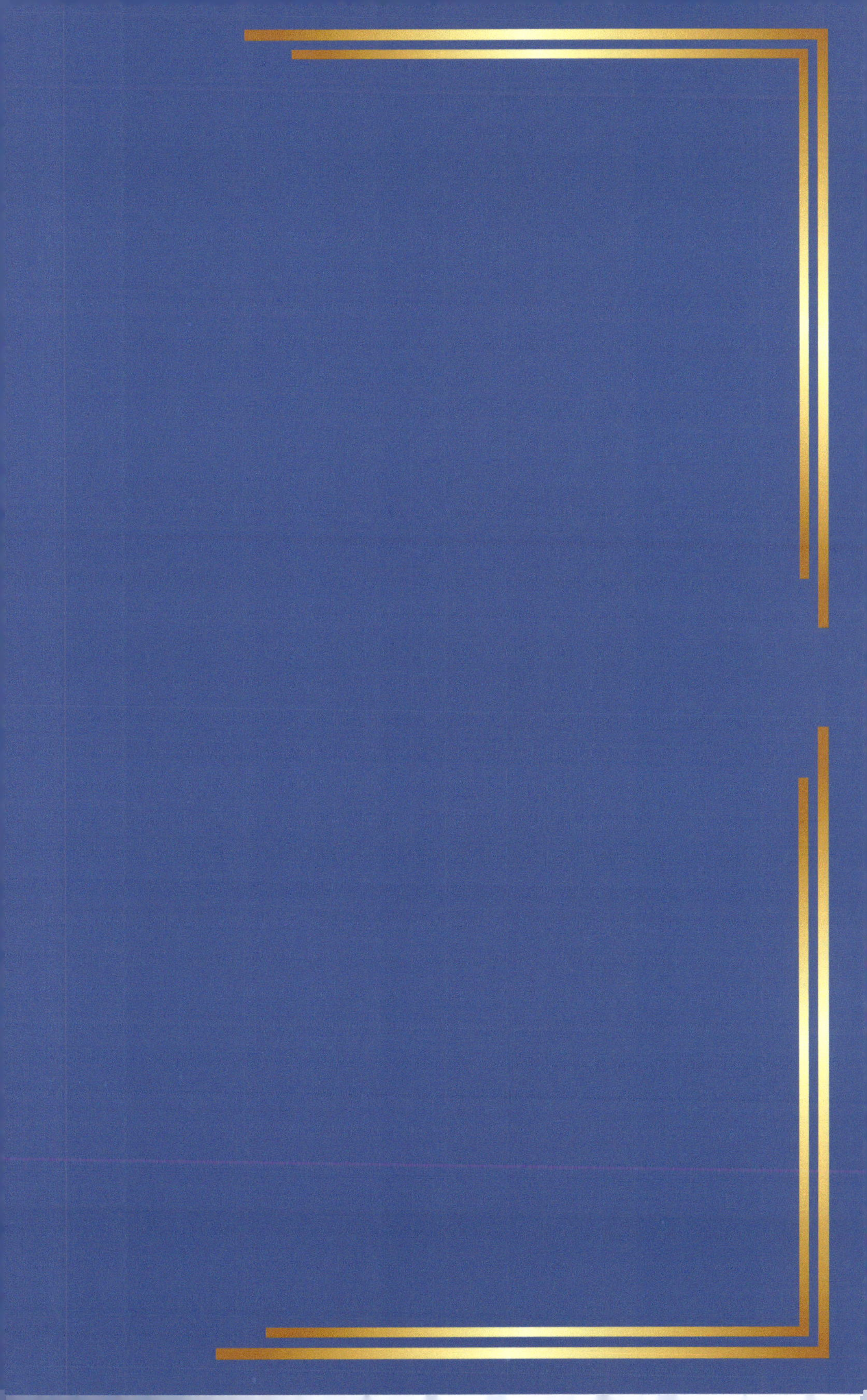

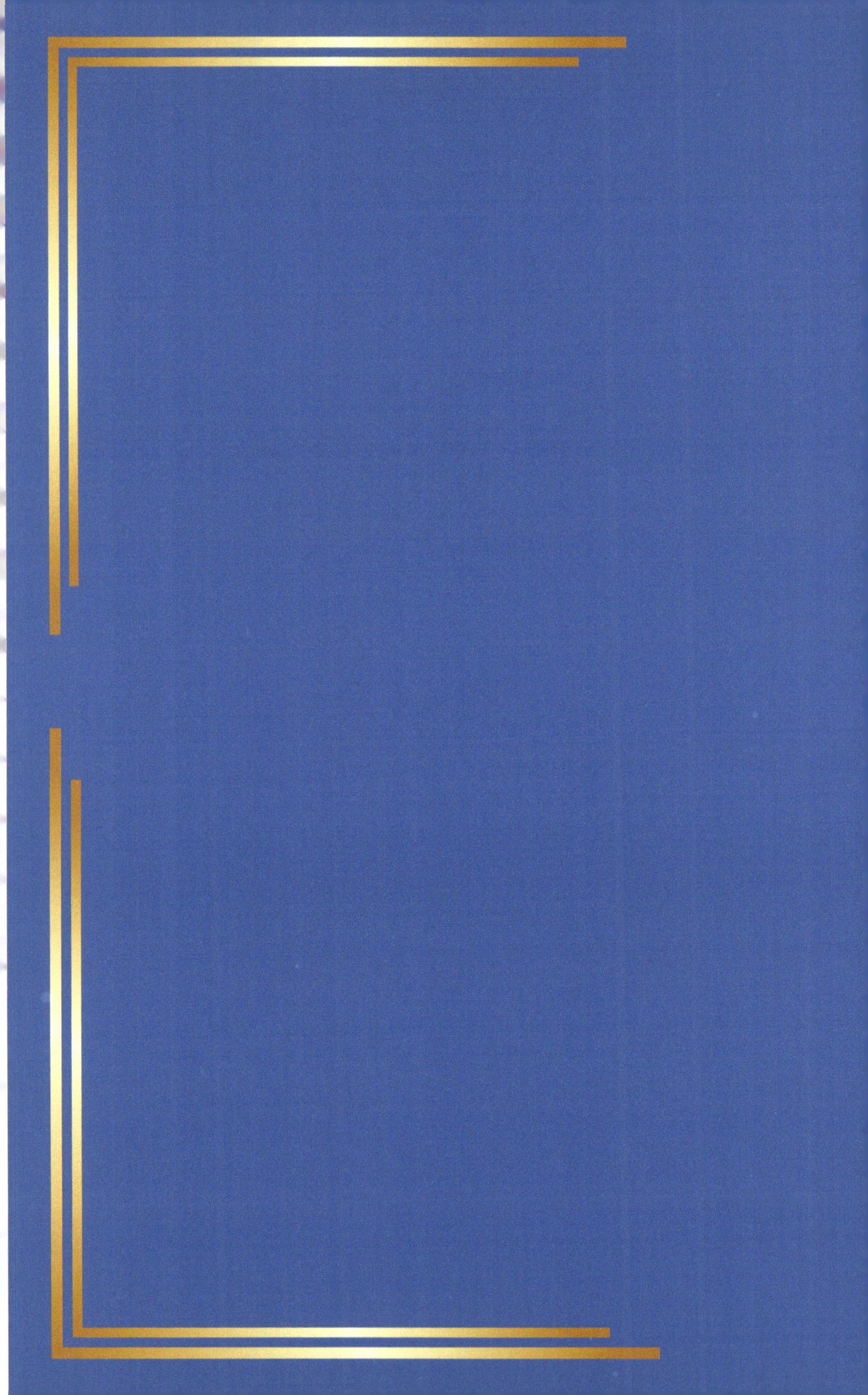

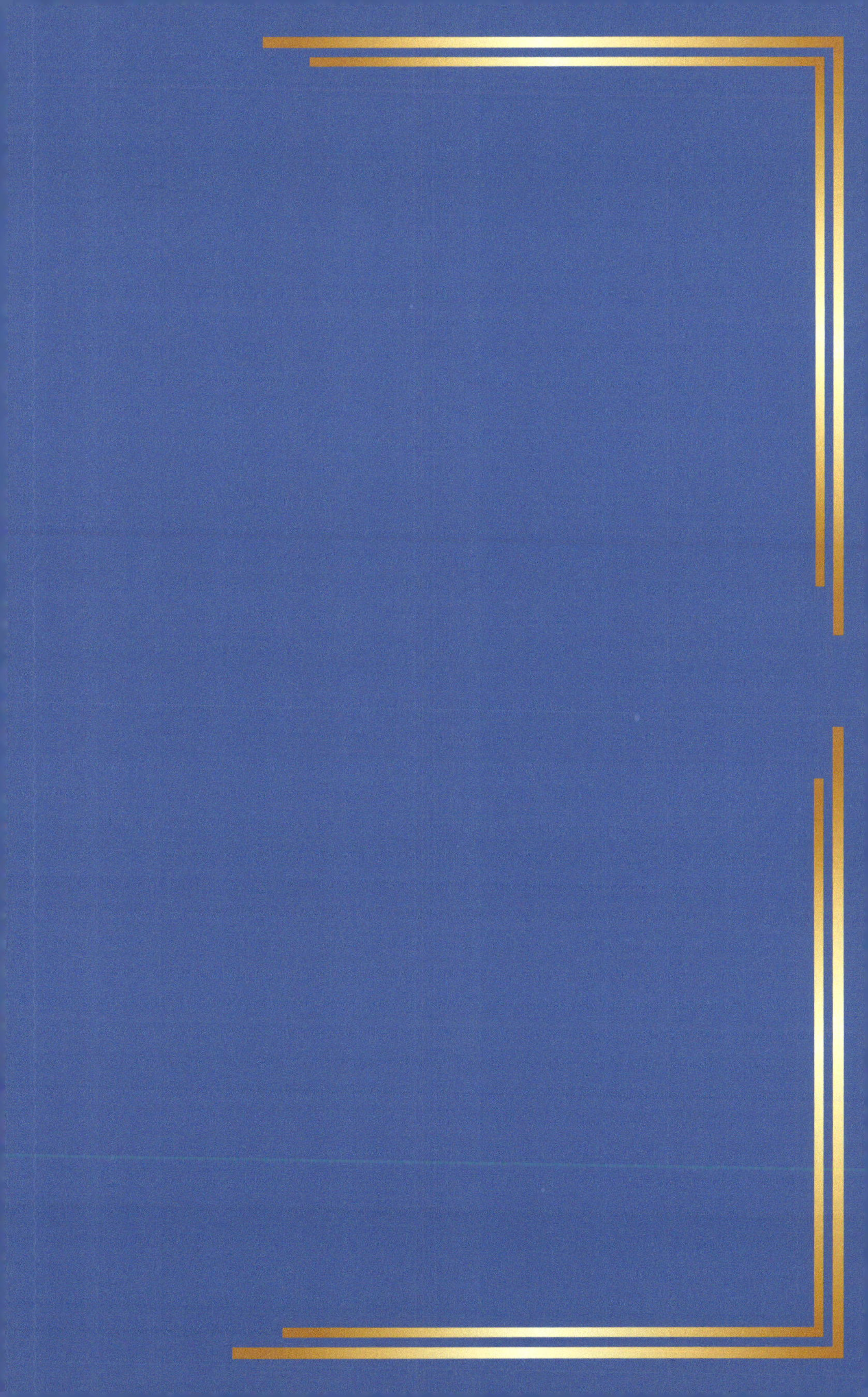

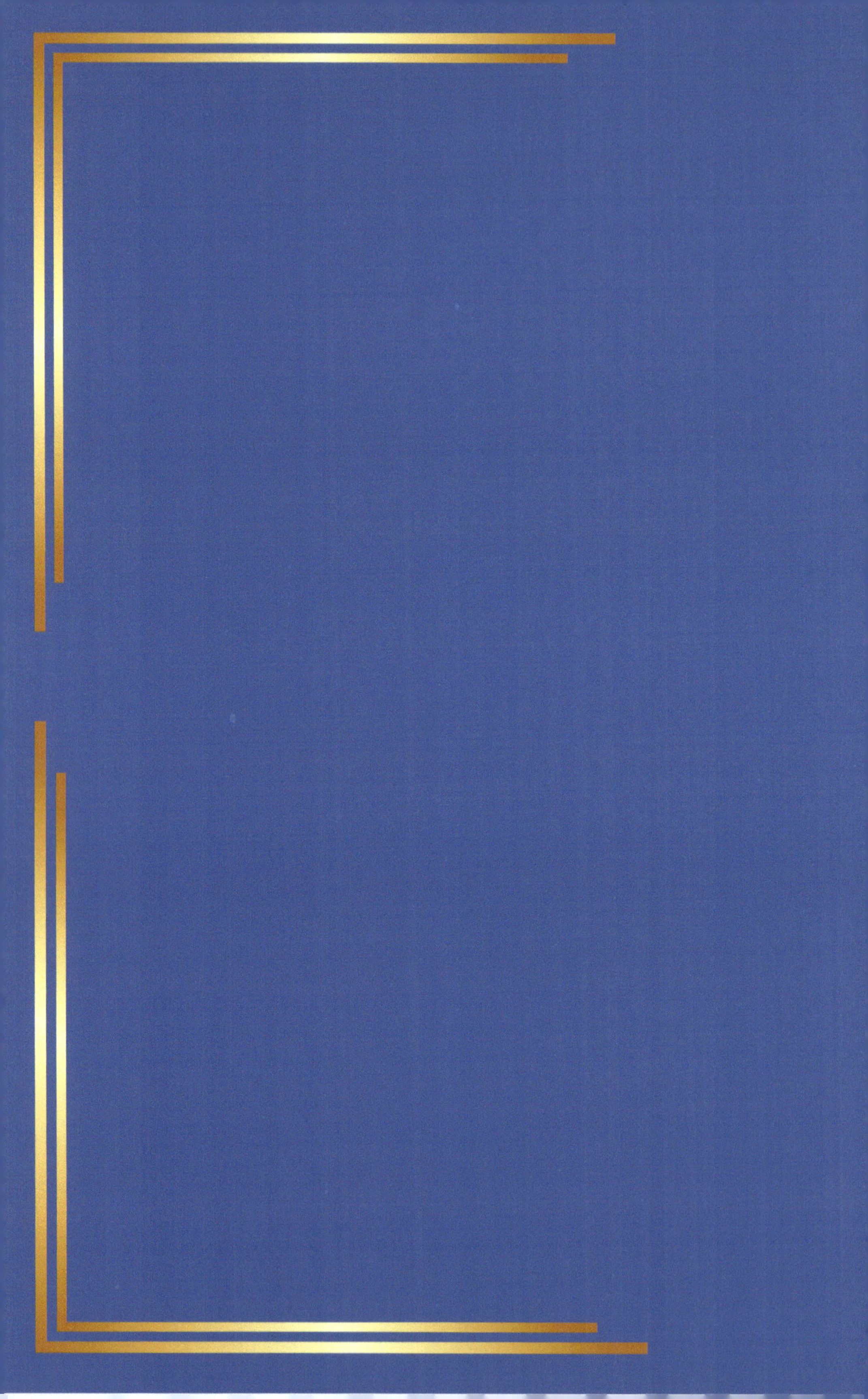

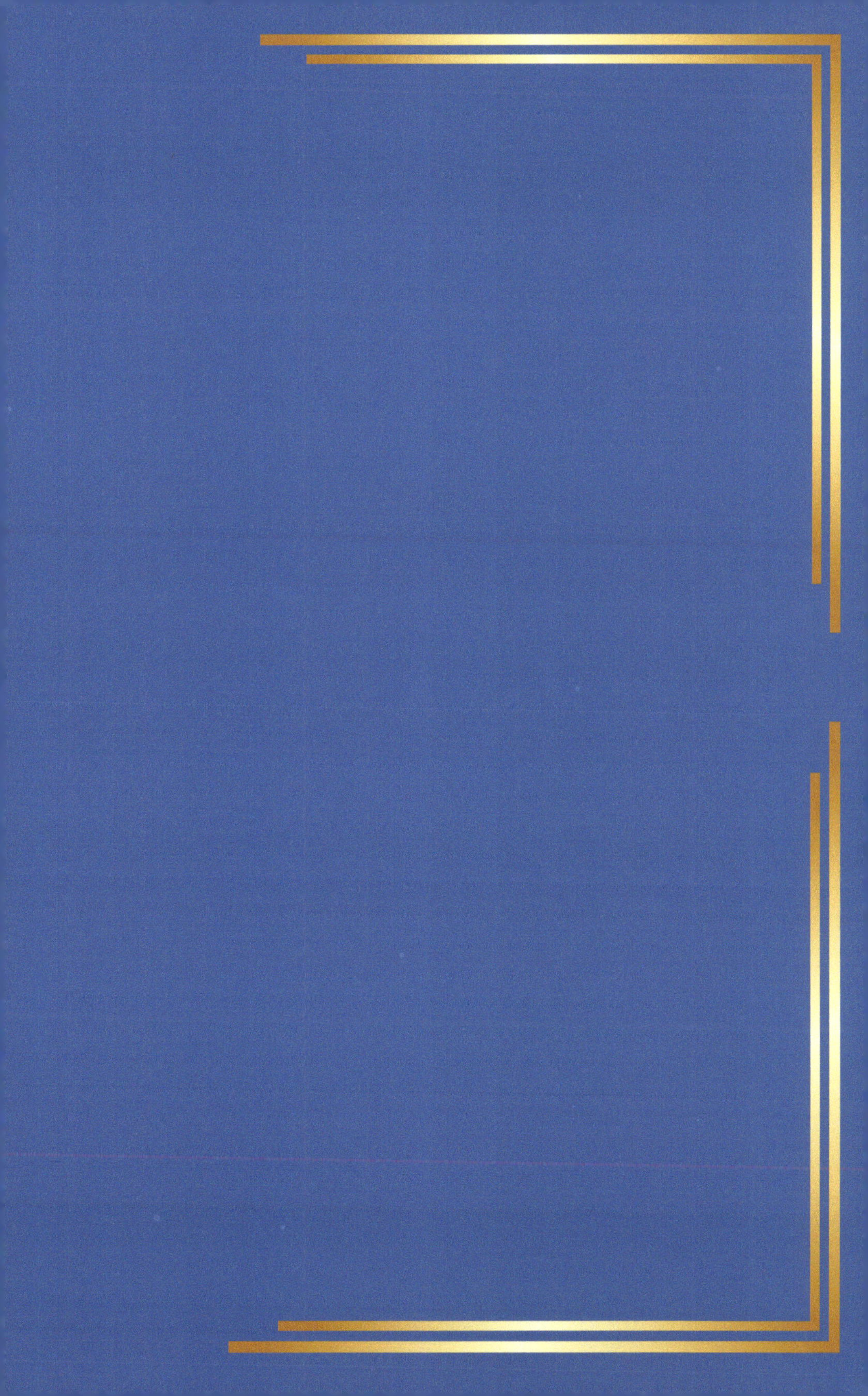

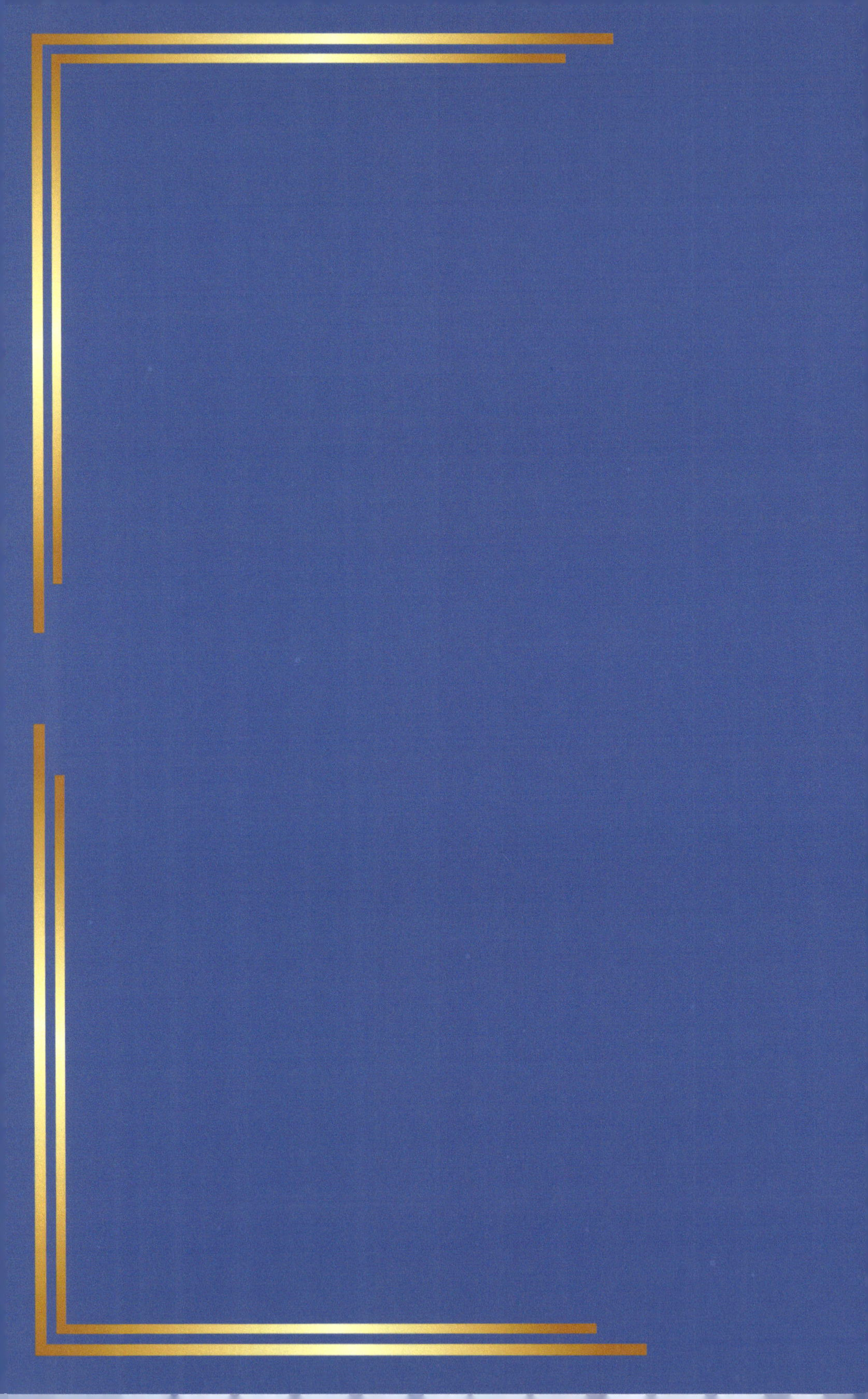

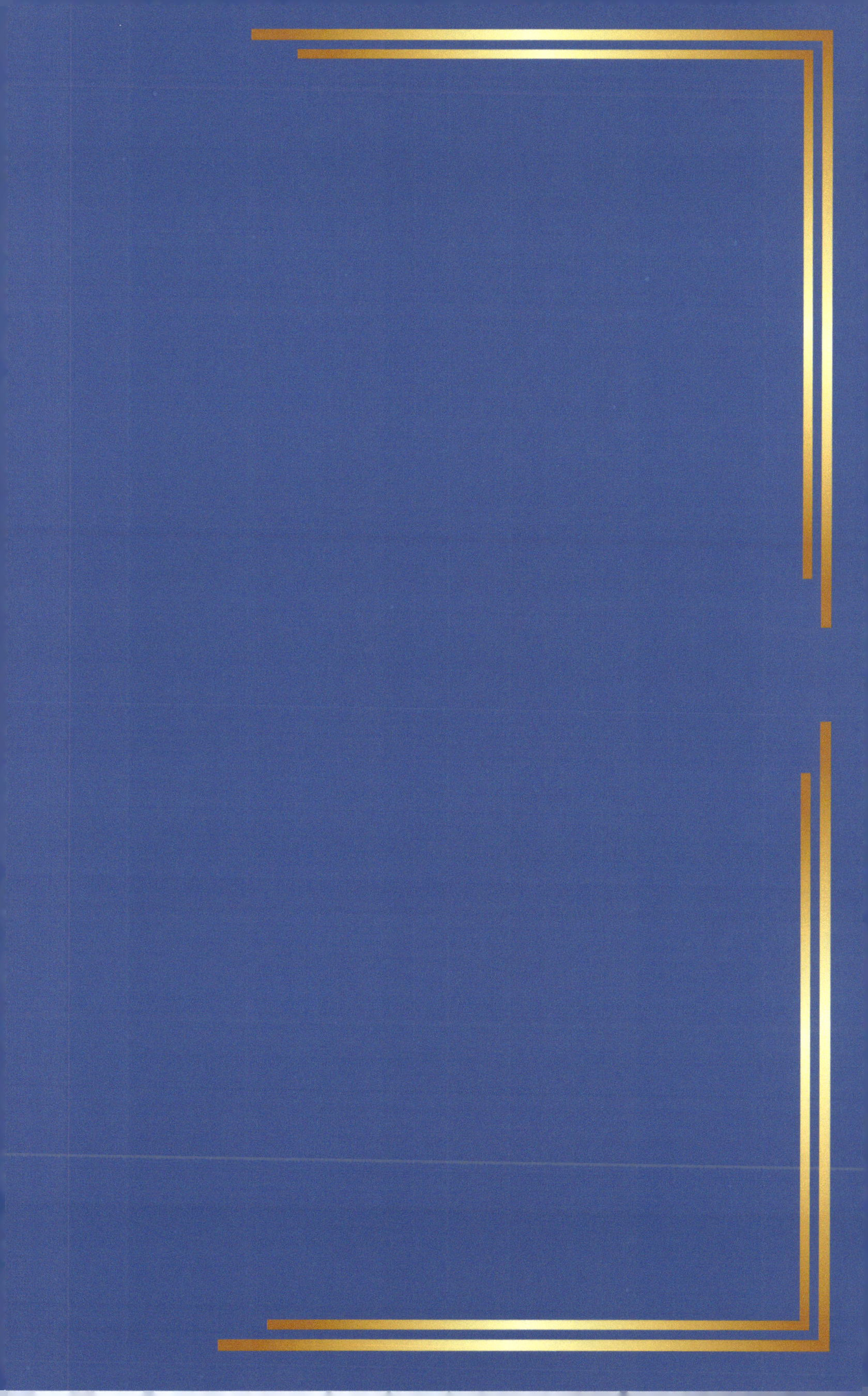

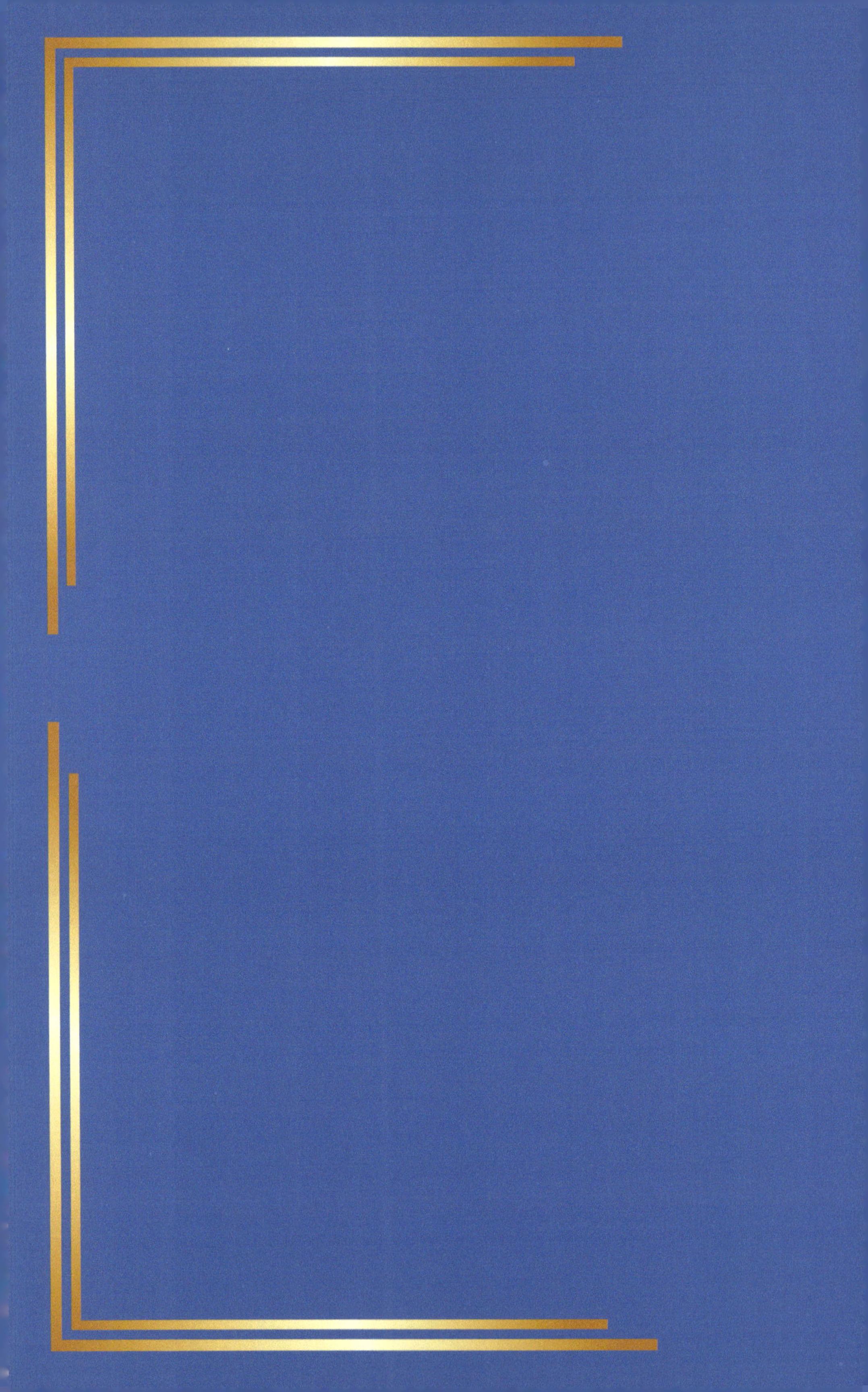

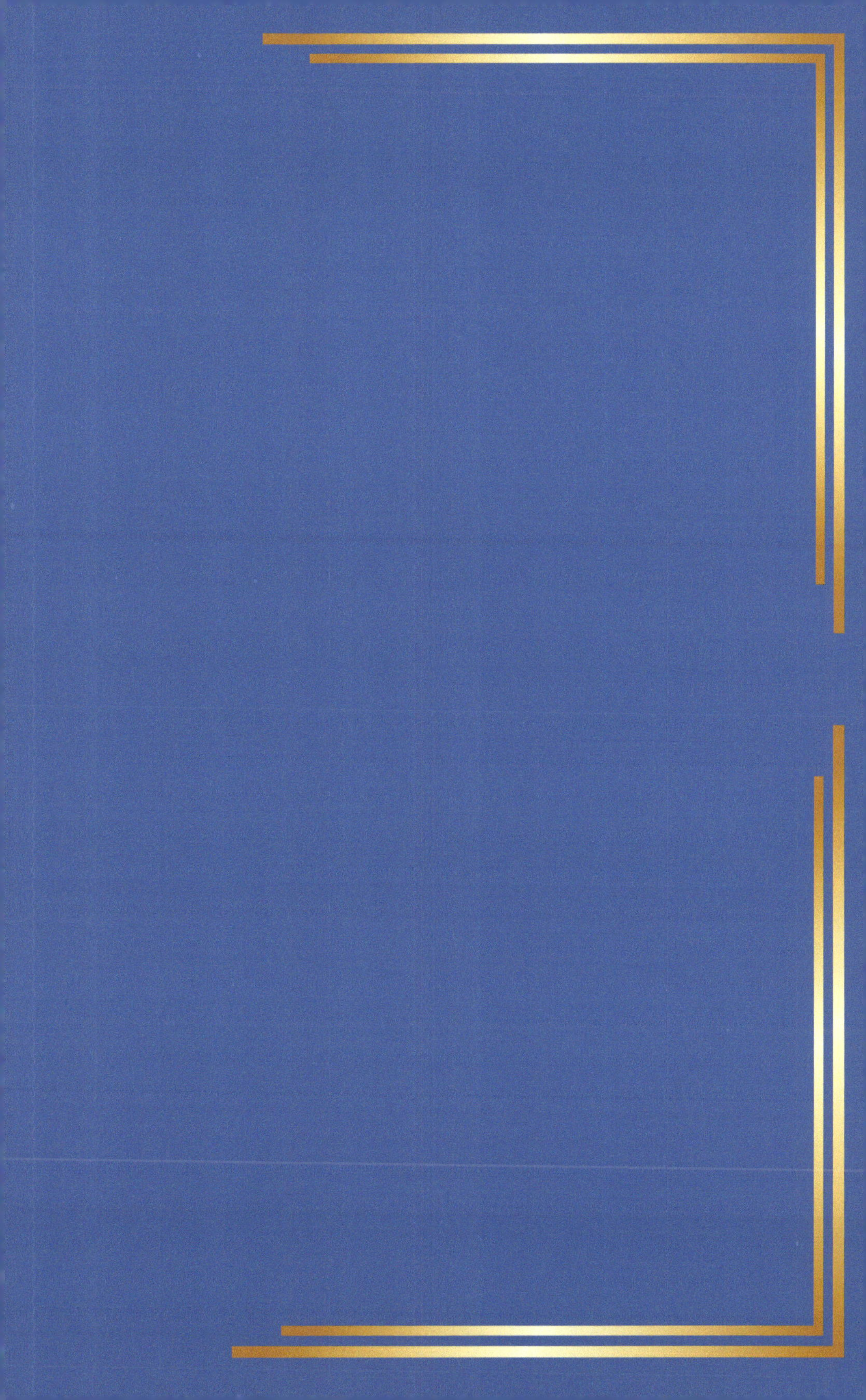

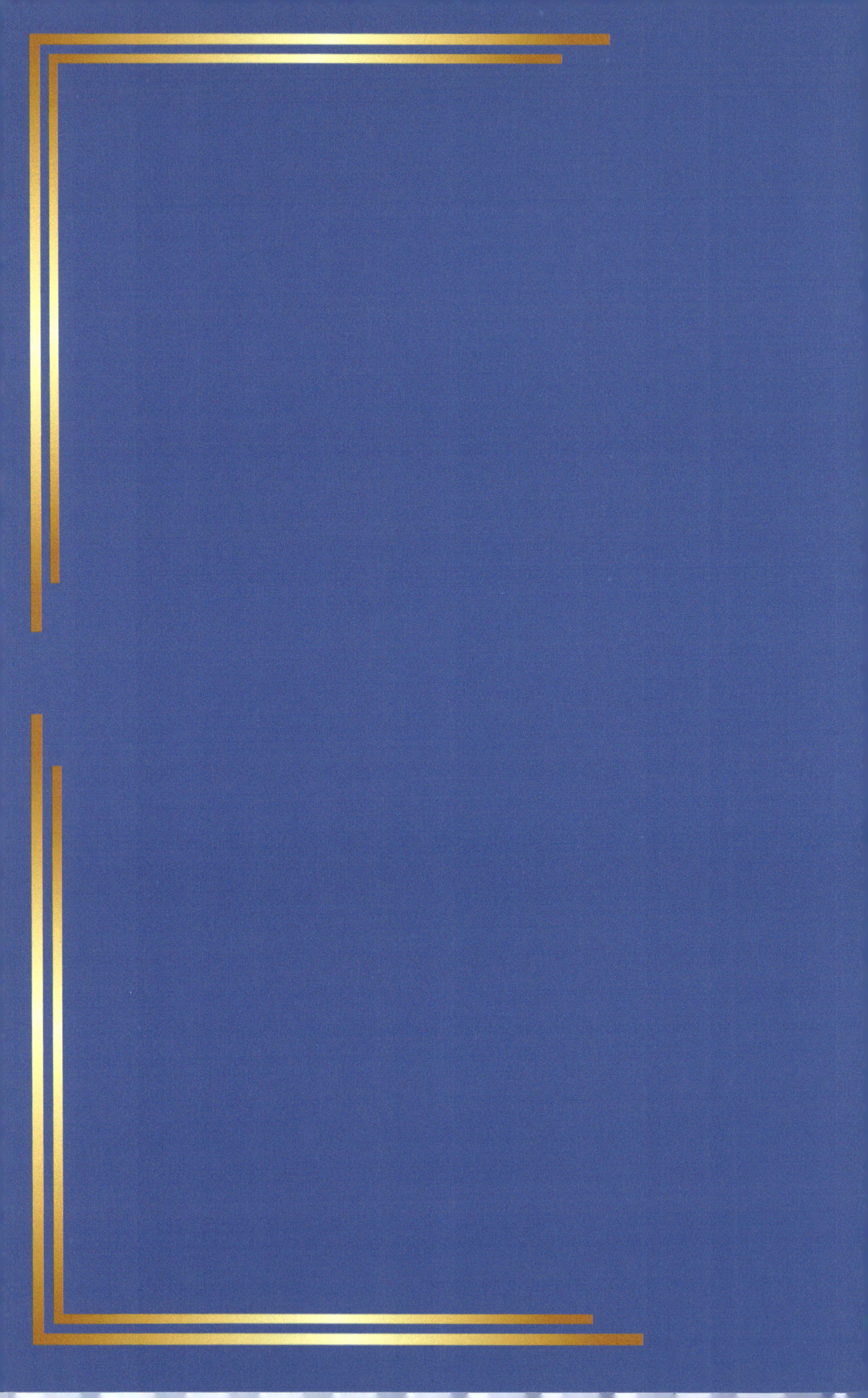

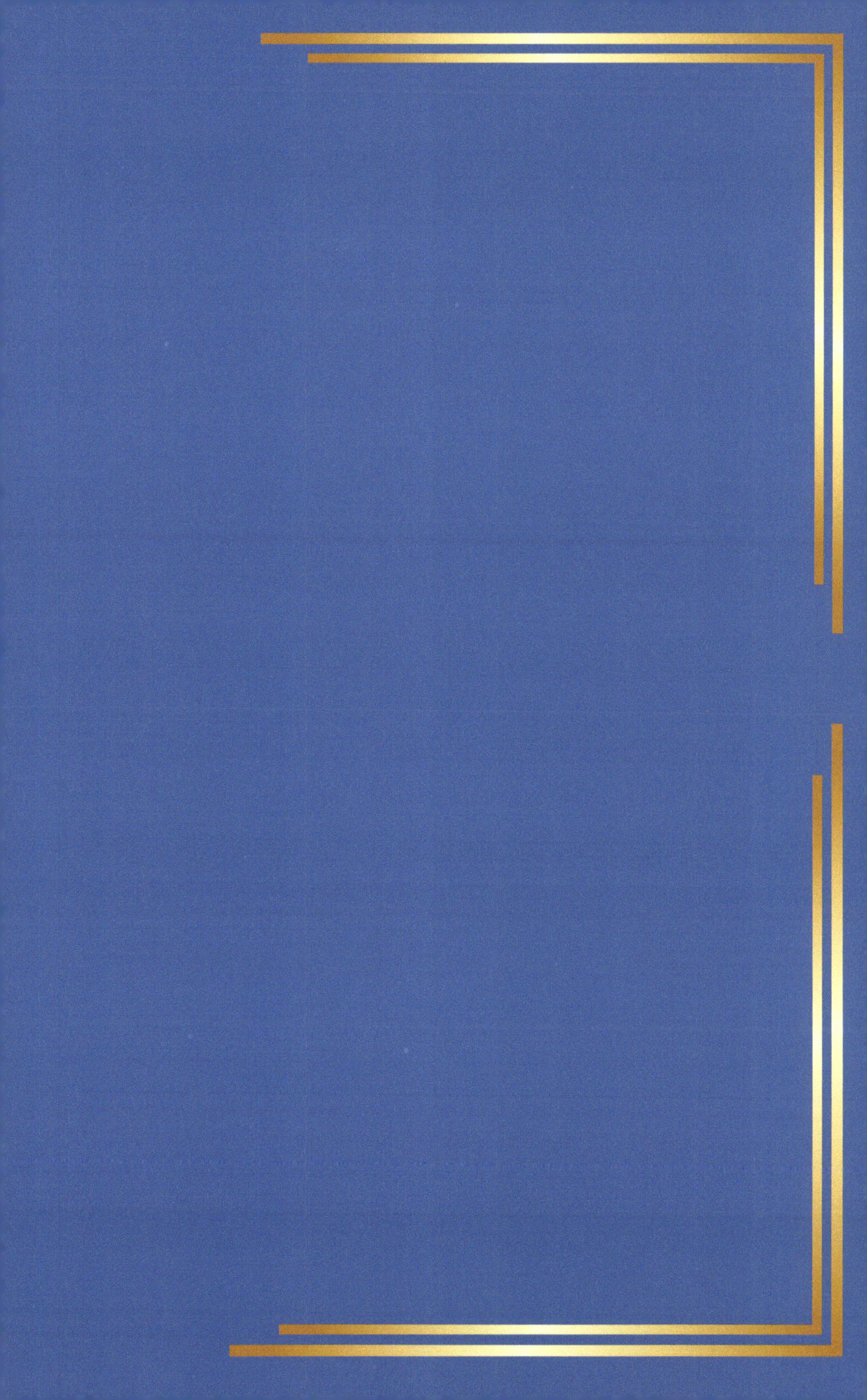

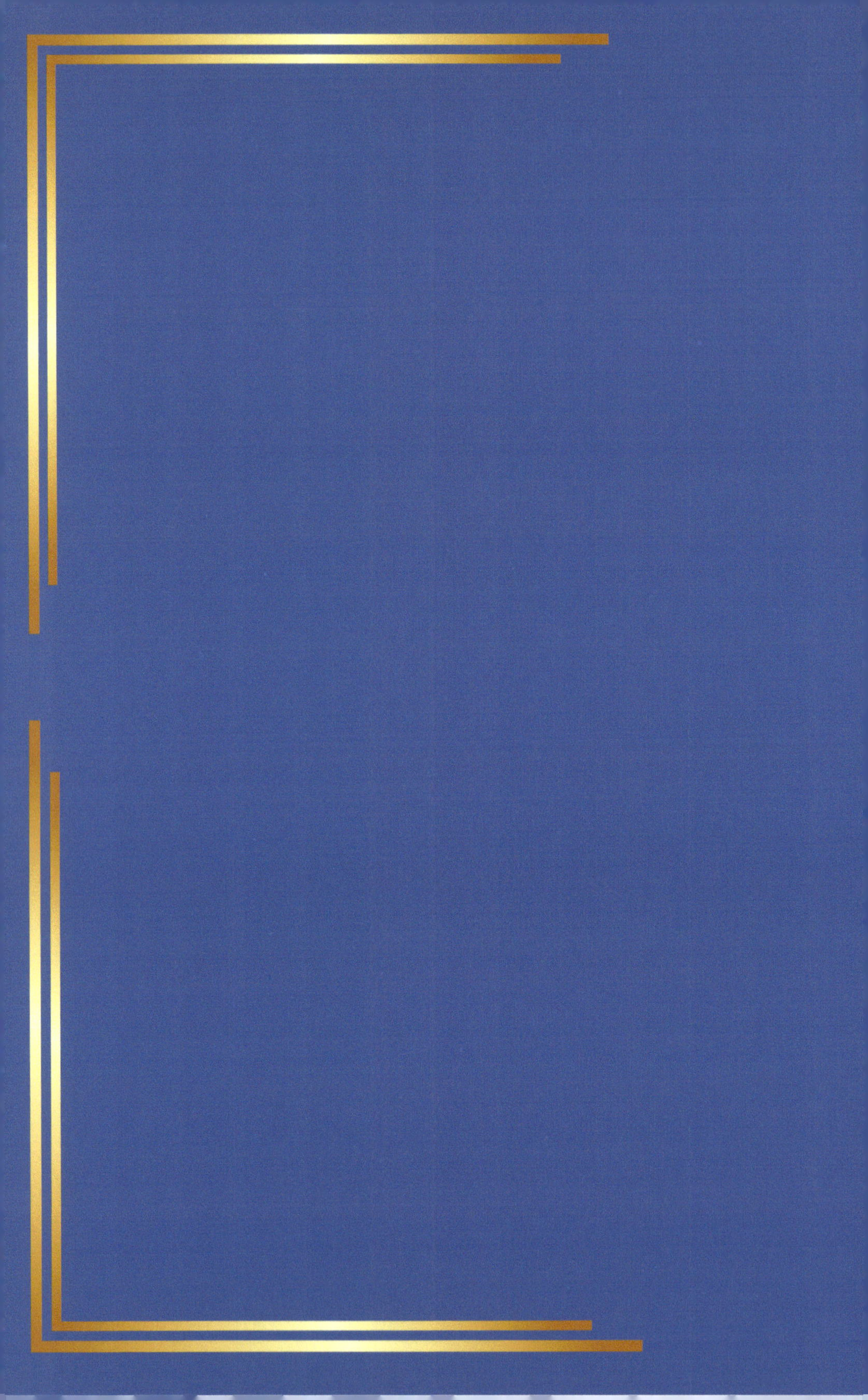

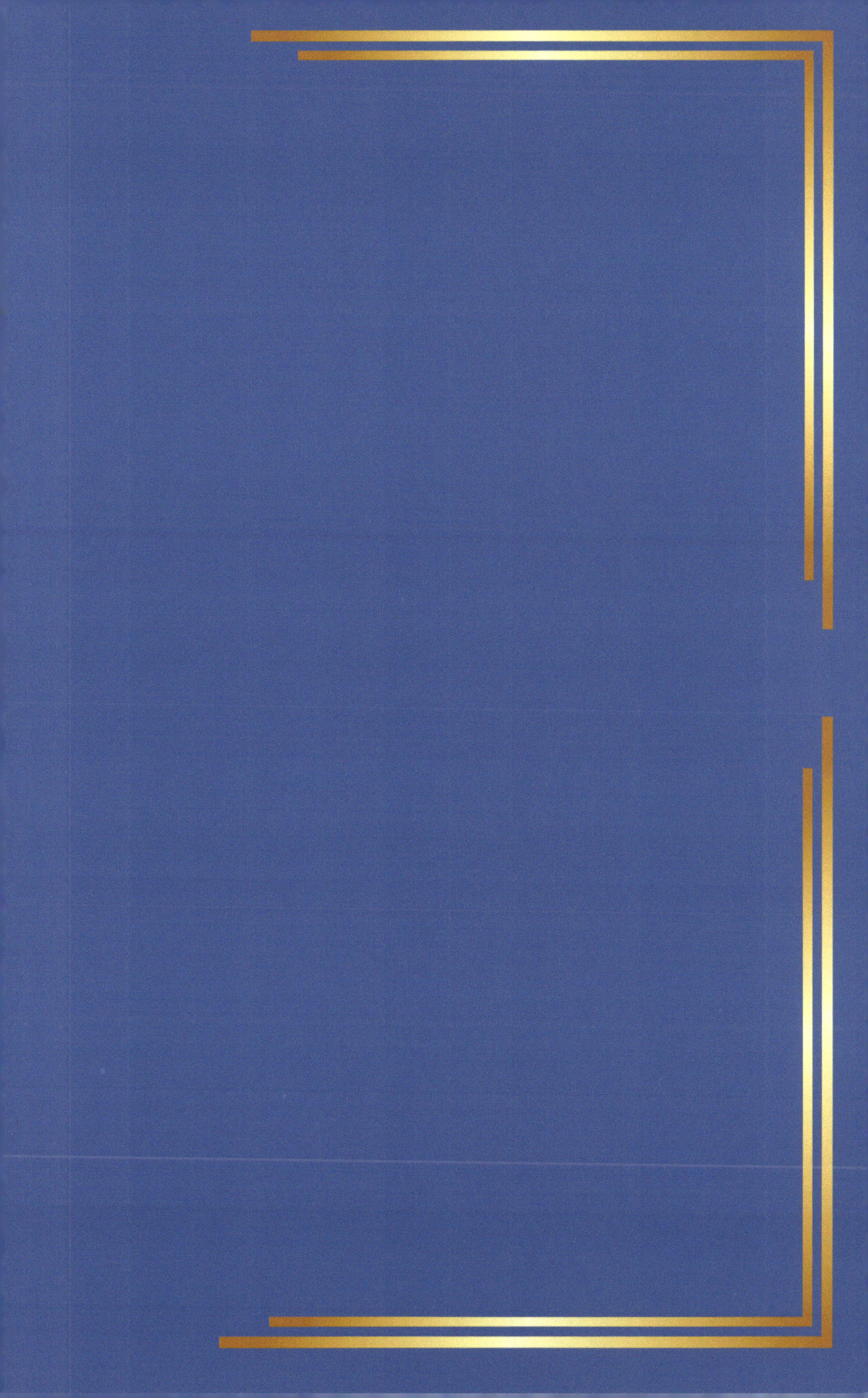

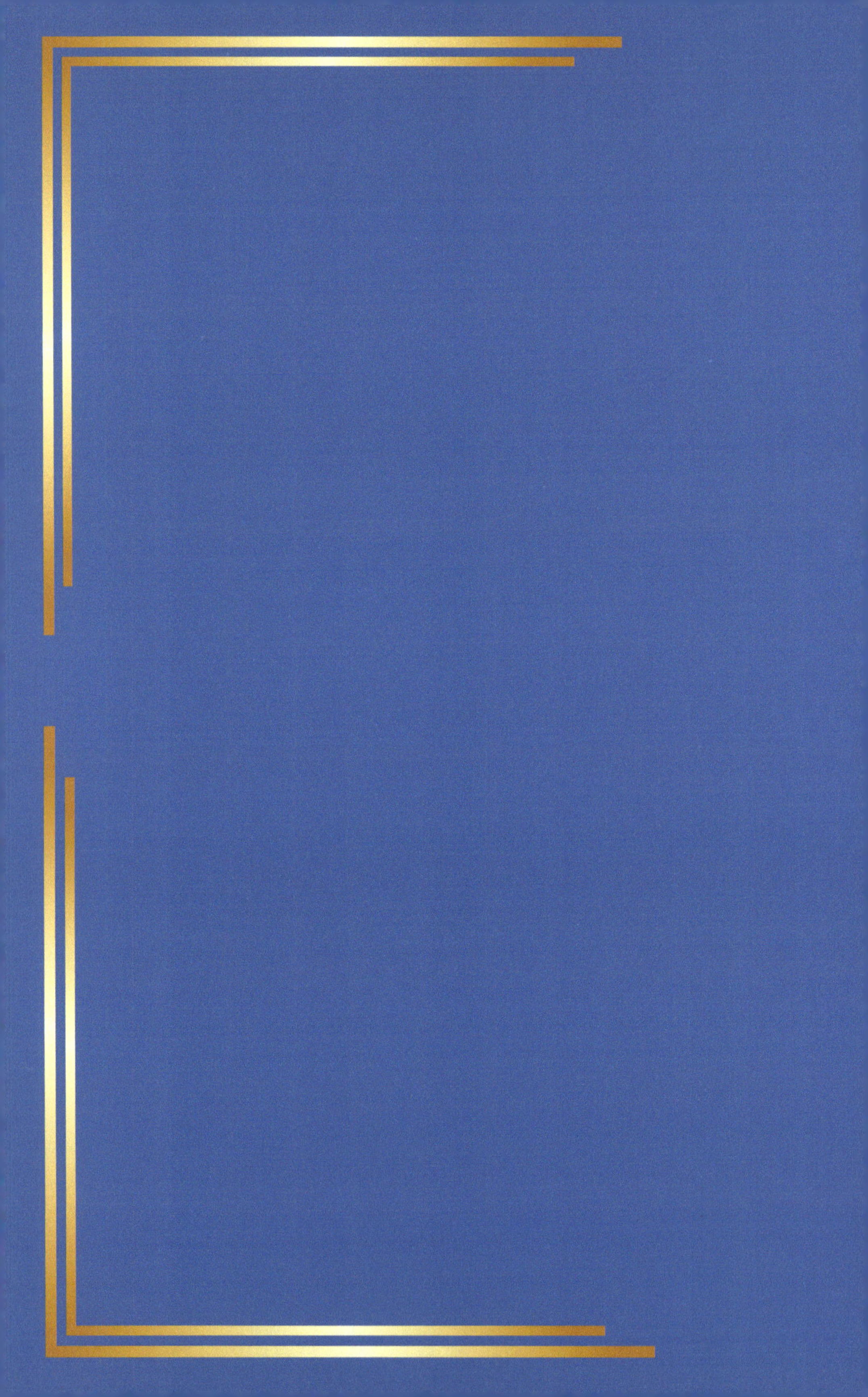

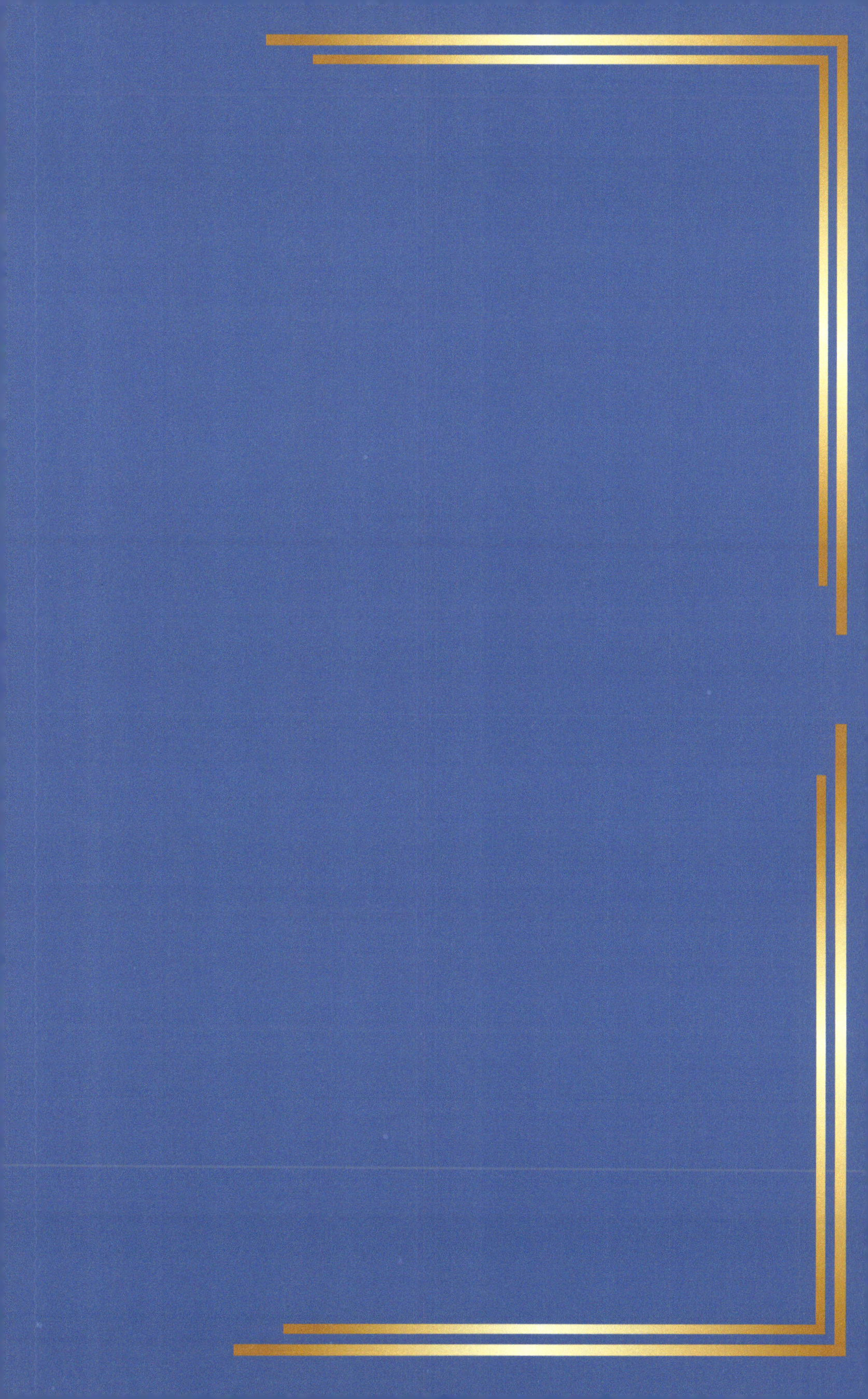

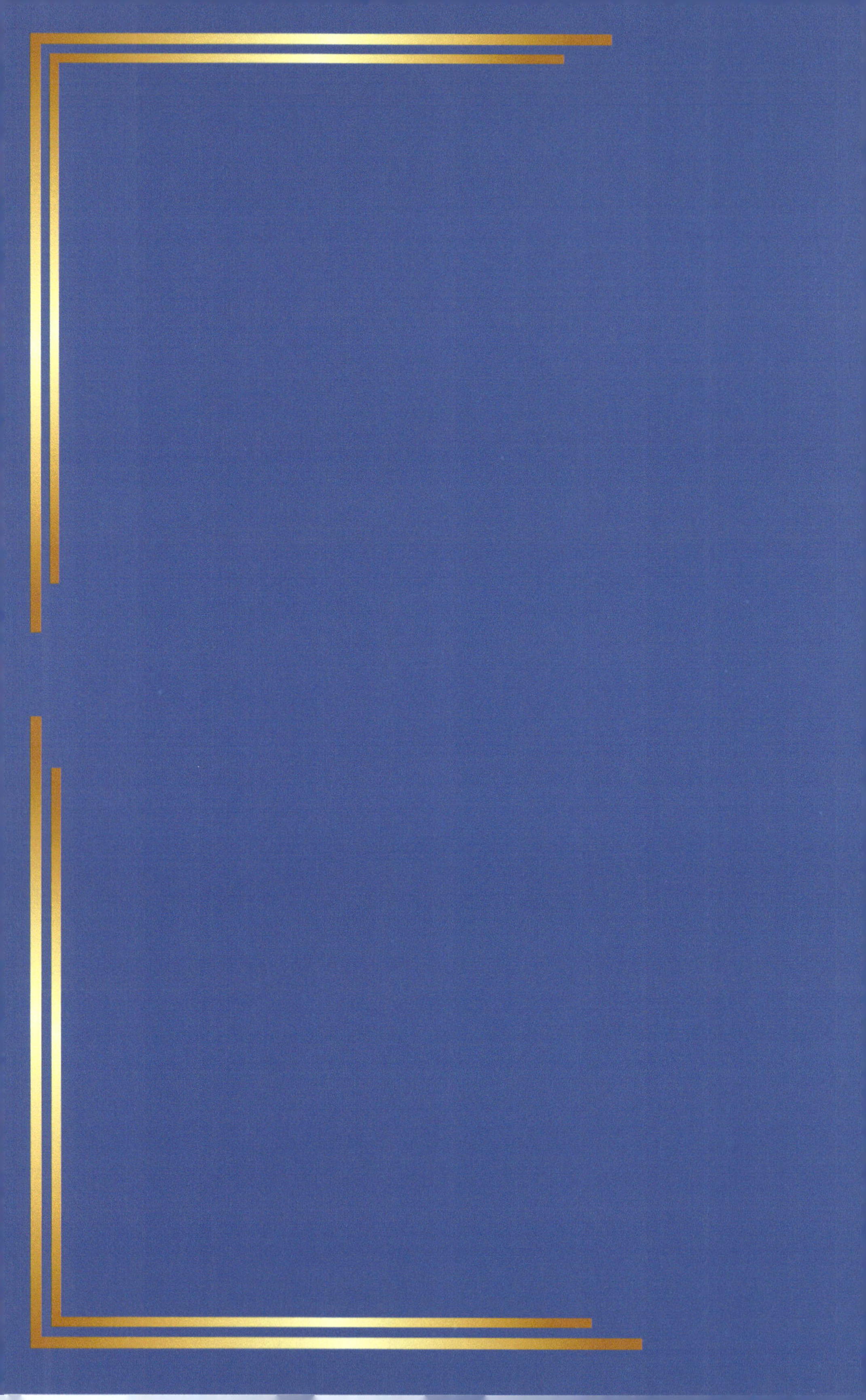

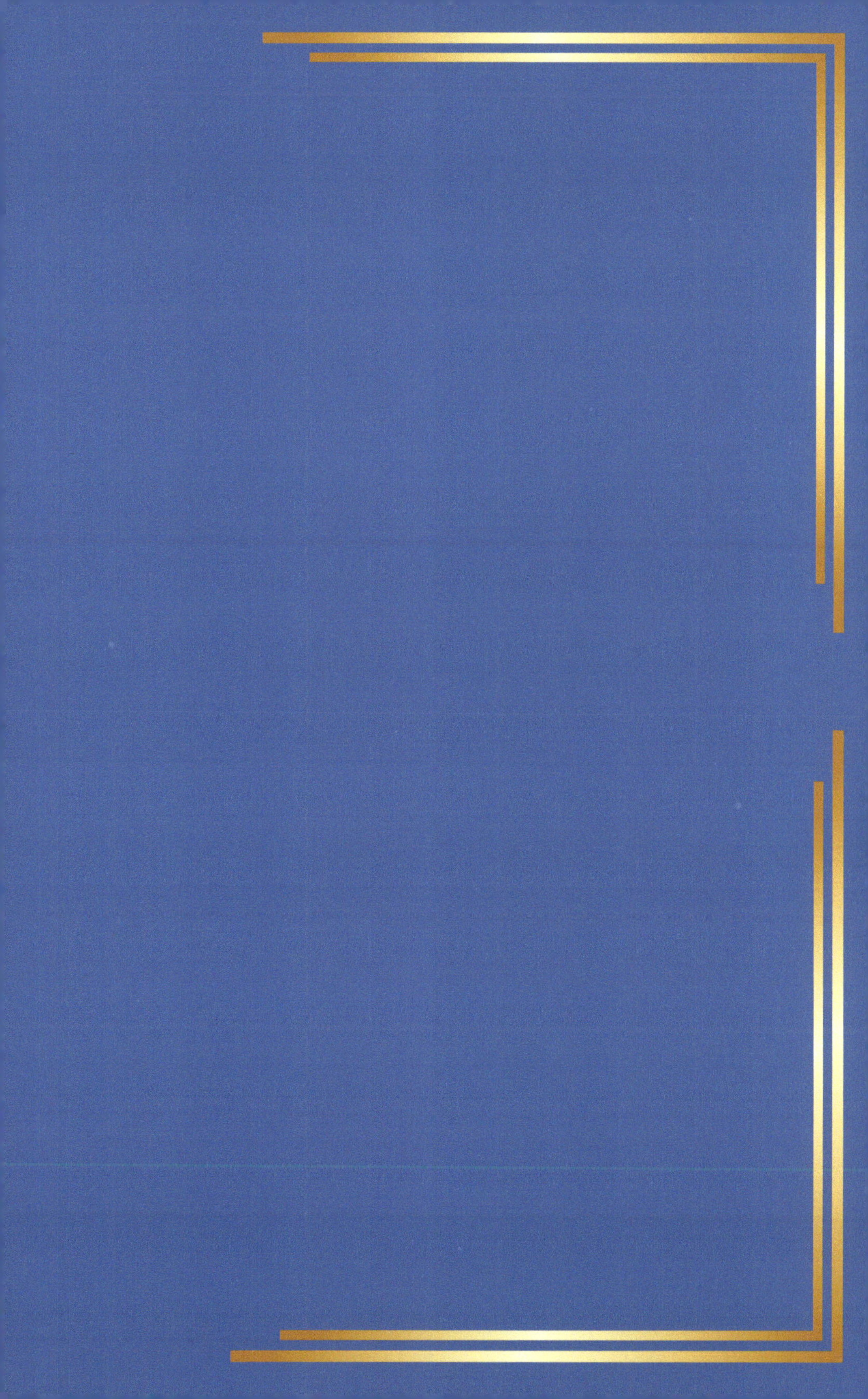

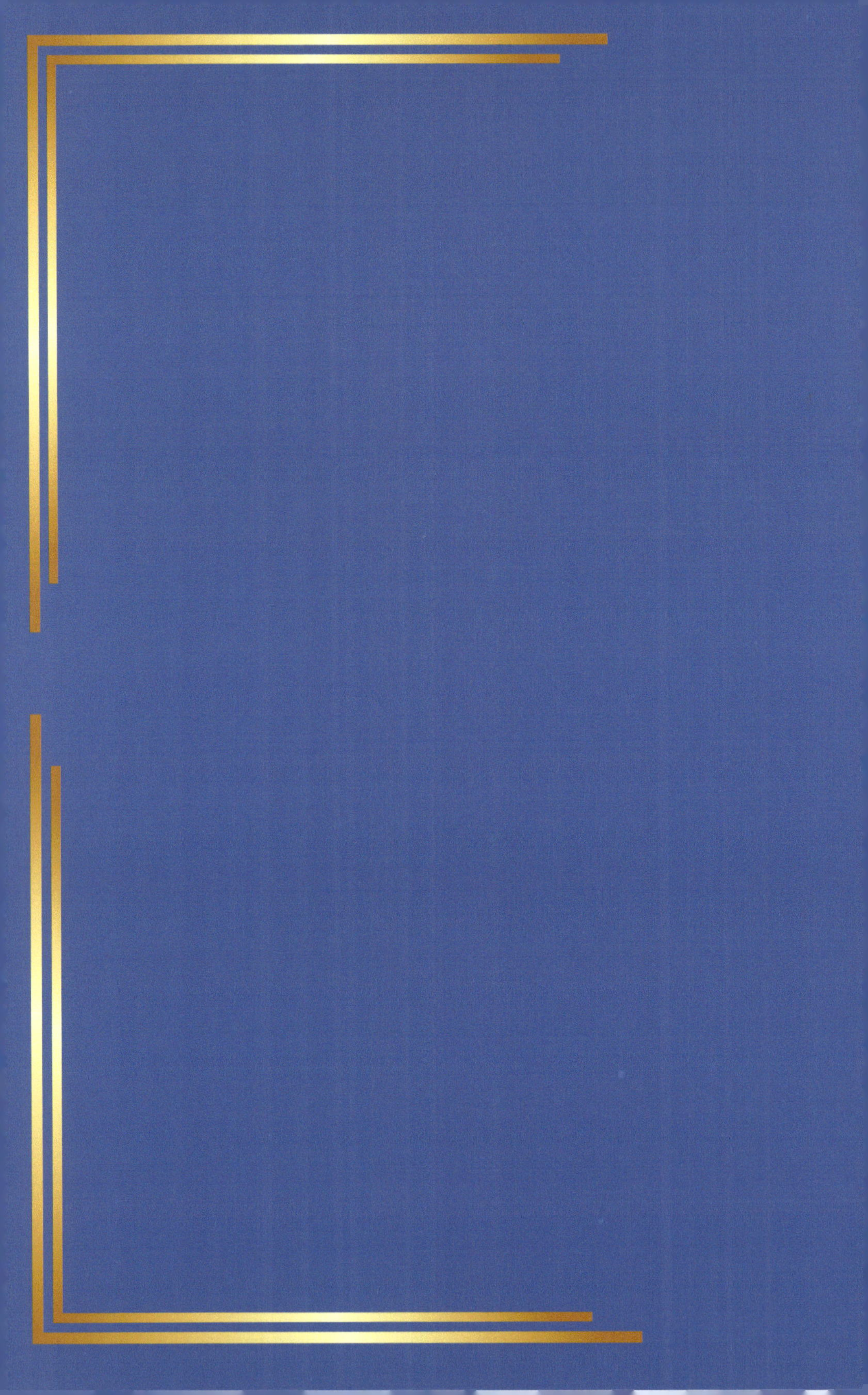

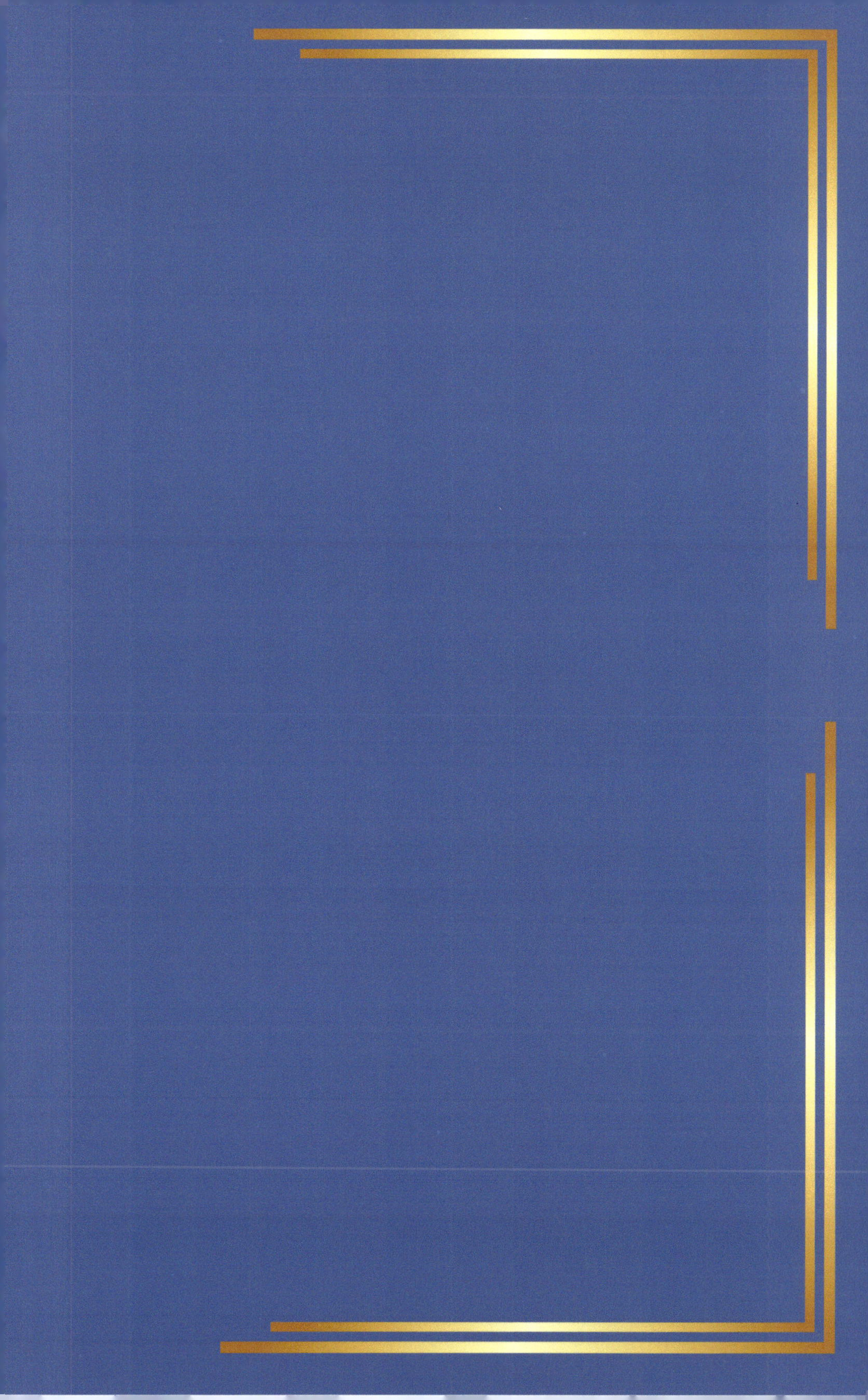

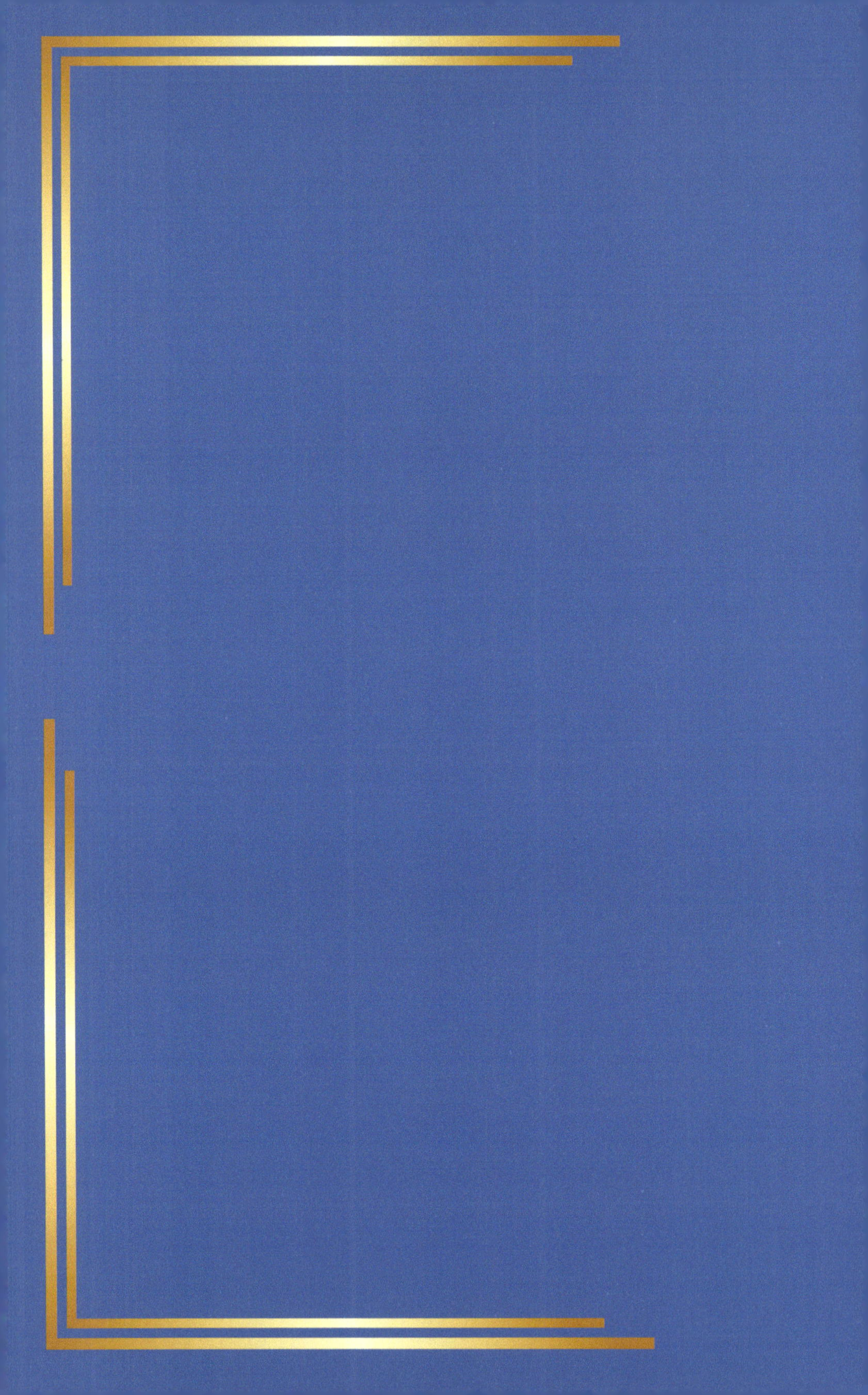

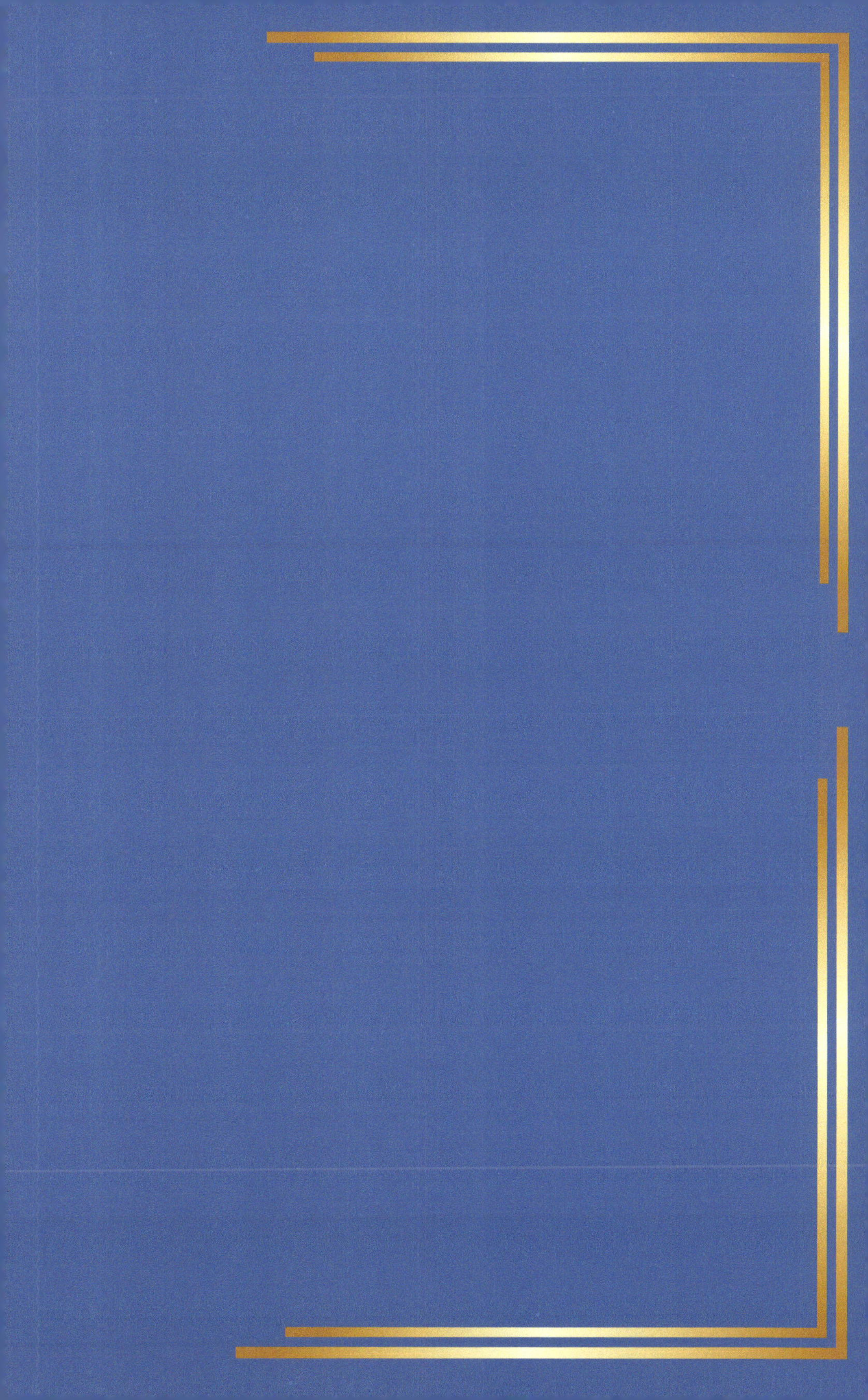

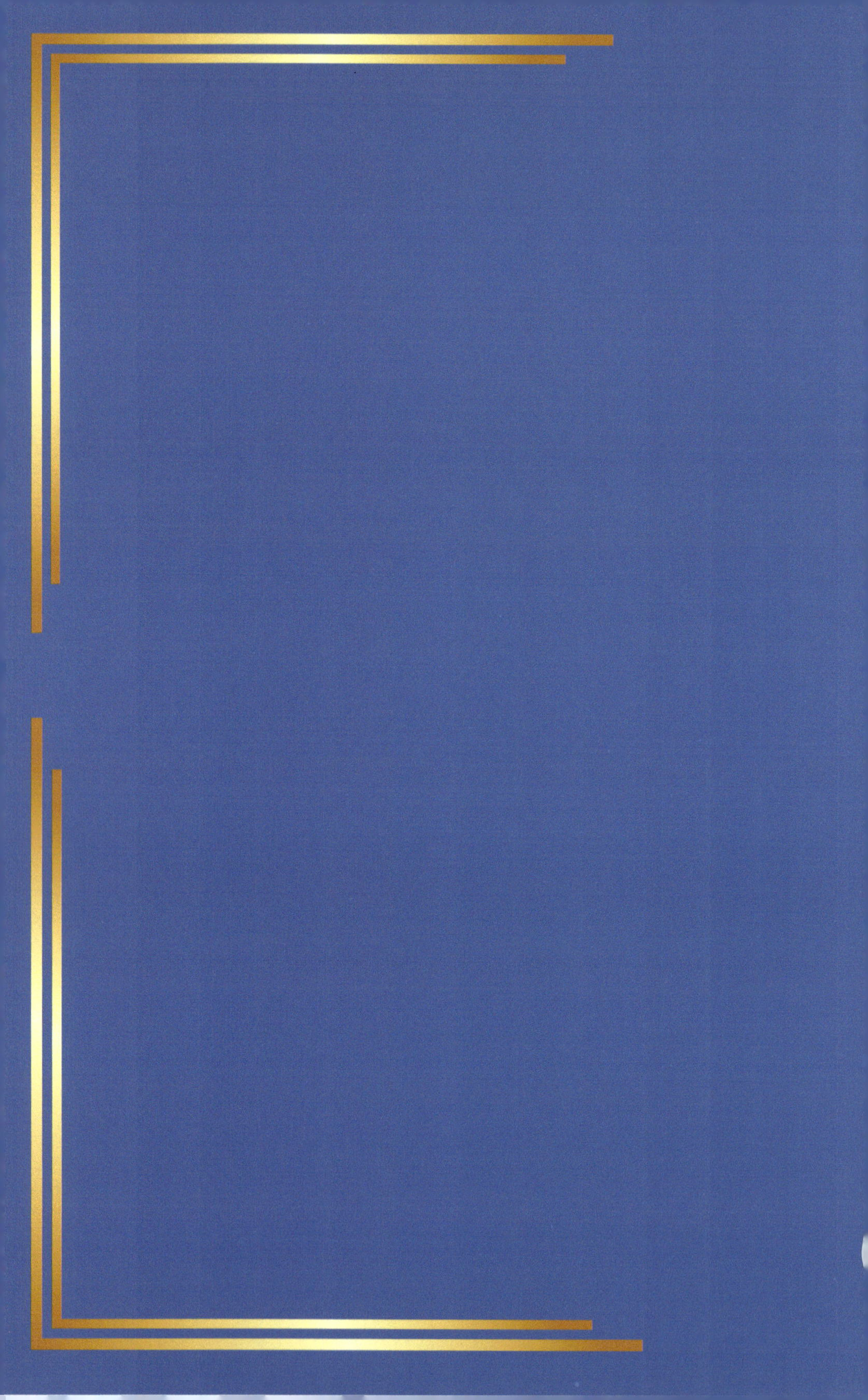

Would you like to enter our monthly drawing for a free book, as well as receive updates on news and promotions? Simply send us your name, email, and address at perennifoliopress@gmail.com and we will enter your name in each month's drawing!

For more updates and opportunities, follow us at:
Website: www.perennifolio.com
Instagram: @perennifoliopress
Facebook: @perennifolio
Linkedin:
www.linkedin.com/perennifolio

www.ingramcontent.com/pod-product-compliance
Lightning Source LLC
LaVergne TN
LVHW052255100826
845147LV00001B/52

* 9 7 9 8 9 0 2 9 0 0 0 4 7 *